BEING A *TIGER!!*

LIFE AND LEADERSHIP LESSONS

Col Harpreet Singh Kohli

PENTAGON PRESS LLP

First published in 2024 by
PENTAGON PRESS LLP
206, Peacock Lane, Shahpur Jat
New Delhi-110049, India
Contact: 011-26490600

Typeset in Palatino, 11 Point
Printed by Aegean Offset Printers, Greater Noida, U.P.

ISBN: 978-81-951894-6-5 (PB)

www.pentagonpress.in

Dedicated to the Memory of

Lt Col Brahmanand Awasthy,

***TIGER,* Fourth Battalion The Rajput Regiment**

His story has been an inspiration ever since I first heard of him and his last stand along with his Rajputs in NEFA on 23 November 1962.

Truly the epitome of what troops would want to see in their Commanding Officer; so much so that they shielded him with their own bodies and happily sacrificed themselves before their TIGER too ultimately fell in the glorious battlefield, right next to them.

CONTENTS

AUTHOR'S NOTE

So we meet again, Dear Reader!

This book had been churning in my mind for most part of the last four years or so since I relinquished the command of my Battalion. I'll attempt to explain the reason why in this short note.

Being a *Tiger* (*Tiger* is the code name for Commanding Officer in the Indian Army) had been a dream ever since I first reported to my Battalion after being commissioned as a young 22-year-old Lieutenant.

The 14½ years thereafter that followed before I got the honour of getting to command my own Battalion were spent learning the ropes in various profiles in field and peace locations while tenanting various regimental and staff tenures as well as a few courses of instruction to build up a holistic professional experience.

This is typical of any officer who joins the Indian Army, as he grows in service with three time-bound promotions till he reaches the rank of Lieutenant Colonel that are more or less assured (barring some extraordinary circumstances, which are rare).

In doing so, the professional performance of officers is judged at various echelons in the chain of command in order to quantify the same before all officers of a particular batch are collectively considered for promotion to the rank of Colonel.

For those selected, the first billet occupied by a newly-promoted Colonel is that of a Commanding Officer of a battalion/regiment.

It is one of the most sacred responsibilities that any officer can hope to be entrusted with - an opportunity to lead 800 men in war and in peace; an opportunity to be a *Tiger* in the true sense of the word!

Anyone who has commanded a battalion will tell you without a second thought that it was the best part of their military career, no matter how long or short it may have been.

In my case, this phase lasted from June 2016 till April 2019.

It was a phase that taught me a *lot*.

It was a phase that made me grow the most - emotionally, professionally as well as spiritually.

It was a phase that taught me many lessons.

It was a phase that set me on a much different course in my life than what would have been otherwise.

But most importantly, it was also a phase that saw me make quite a few mistakes. Mistakes which ultimately made me into what I am today, with the benefit of the nearly three years' experience as a *Tiger.*

I learnt the ropes with a whole bunch of people to guide and mentor me, which they did with the best of intentions in their hearts. But as they say, no single template fits all situations. The same was the case here as well.

They knew that all they could offer was advice, based

on what their own experiences had taught them. And in a very short time, I too found out that even the best intentioned advice from a predecessor, or even a peer, could at best, only show you the path.

Ultimately, it was you yourself who had to actually tread that path and see what lay ahead!

As I mentioned above, I'll be wrong if I say it was all smooth sailing, or that I didn't make any mistakes in my journey as a Commanding Officer, or a *Tiger,* as my call-sign was. However, as I realized over time, it was these mistakes that played a key role in me maturing in my new role as the head of the family for 800 souls.

It was these mistakes that taught me some really valuable lessons about life and leadership, that are not only relevant to a military man but, instead, to anyone in any position of authority over any number of men or women.

Hence, the decision to write this book, with a sincere hope that at least one person may learn from my mistakes and *not* make the same when it is their time to lead.

I will consider this book a success if that happens.

1

THE BEGINNING: GETTING INTO THE 'HOT' CHAIR

Taking Over the Baton

Looking back nearly six years after the events that I am about to relate here happened, I am all smiles!

Having sat on the 'hot' chair for almost three years, and writing this particular part of the book another two years after that, all I can say is that it was perhaps the most satisfying phase of my life. I don't think anything that will come my way in life can ever match the high that I rode on for those three years, commanding those 800-odd individual souls who, together, are some of the best soldiers that there can be. So much so that after relinquishing command, I even wrote on my social media account - 'The Work of My Life is Done'.

But then, I hardly knew it during the days leading up to my getting to that chair! Here is how the days immediately preceding, and succeeding that moment went by.

I had spent the bulk of the years 2013 to 2015 in a mighty busy appointment, with a highly demanding boss in the second half. Hence, when I got my orders to proceed for the Senior Command Course in November 2015 and report to my battalion after that, I was a much relieved man. November was still three months away though, and there were two major professional events lined up prior to my move, thereby ensuring that there was practically no breathing space before the course commenced.

But then, that's the way life had been for the past two years plus and being purely professional commitments, the two-week long, 18-20-hour days before I finally left were gladly faced and, dare I say, it was a job well done at the end of it all to everyone's satisfaction. That done, I rushed home for a quick two-day layover at home in Delhi and the next day I found myself in the small town of Mhow.

The Senior Command Course is aimed at guiding potential Commanding Officers of the Indian Army. Having done fairly okay in my career thus far, I was reasonably sure that my name would eventually figure in the list of those approved to become Colonels when it was the turn of my batch to be promoted and hence my nomination for this course.

Anyhow, having just moved on from that really busy appointment, I spent the two-month long Senior Command Course trying to catch up with all that lost sleep of the past two years! That apart, the only thing that got my undivided attention was what was called *Command Guidance*.

Of course, no single template can be applied when it comes to commanding troops who hail from practically every part of the country, as well as some from Nepal! So the Command Guidance module was mostly about technical aspects about running the affairs of the battalion, though liberally sprinkled with hands-on command experience of the instructors entrusted with the task of teaching, or rather, guiding us.

Thus ended the Senior Command Course and after a three-week leave, I landed back in my battalion at its then location somewhere in the foothills of Bhutan, after having been away for more than 32 months.

My immediate appointment was that of Battalion 2iC, or the Second in Command. With the then Commanding Officer, Colonel Chandran, having been in command for more than three-and-a-half years, the Battalion was well set in its peacetime routine as per his requirements and directions. So all that was needed of me at that point in time was to get to feel the pulse of the battalion after having been away for so long, and settle into my new responsibility. Having known the boys as well as the Commanding Officer for so long, it did not take long for me to find my rhythm and get on with the job.

I was back home, finally!

Yes, the battalion was my home. I still remember that particular day as a young Lieutenant, the youngest officer of the battalion at that time, when the battalion was in Dehradun sometime in 2003. A veteran who had served for about five years in the army before quitting and migrating abroad, was staying in the Officers' Mess and being the only bachelor present in the battalion at that time, I was all that he had by the way of company over dinner.

At one point in our conversation he somewhat cynically remarked as to what was there to look forward in the army or the unit, hinting indirectly at his own decision to quit after serving for five years.

To this day I don't know how, but I still remember that my reply was instantaneous. *"For the next 20 years at least, this battalion is my home, Sir, and I don't care much for anything beyond that"*, I had replied. Stumped, he had no answer and the topic of our conversation soon changed.

So yes, I was back home indeed.

Home, with hundreds of brothers and their families who were and continue to be, equally dear to me. Home, to the battalion that had time and again, distinguished itself in war as well as in peace. Home, to one of the very few battalions of the Indian Army to have earned both the highest gallantry awards, in war as well as peace – the Param Vir Chakra as well as the Ashok Chakra.

As I said, it was good to be back!

Anyhow, back to my journey towards the 'HOT' seat!

It was somewhat of a foregone conclusion that I would succeed Col Chandran as the next *Tiger* of the battalion, even though the *Selection Board* that decides who become Colonels, at least in respect of my particular batch, was delayed.

Yet, Col Chandran was one visibly relaxed man as he saw the writing on the wall and started gently guiding me towards assuming command of the battalion when my turn came. The first thing he did towards this end was to promptly proceed on leave for almost a month, leaving me to officiate in lieu!

This left me in de facto command of the battalion. It was the first time in my career that I was officiating in the Commanding Officer's absence. But then, not only were various drills already in place as per Col Chandran's directions, fact was that it was still he who was the Commanding Officer, even if he was on leave! Why I say so is because the happenings in the battalion were still *his* responsibility, regardless of his physical presence or lack of it.

The Buck ALWAYS Stops with the Tiger, as they say in the Indian Army.

As I move on, I think it is worth mentioning that life in the Indian Army, and command of a battalion is much more than just a 9-to-5 job. With 800 men under your command, resolution of any issue created by any one of them, professional or personal, including on the domestic front, is the responsibility of the Commanding Officer. Period.

You may wonder why domestic issues come under this purview as well. The fact is that for a soldier to be able to focus solely on the job of soldiering, he has to be free of distractions or worries, especially related to family because in many cases, he cannot be physically present with them always.

Command of troops is an onerous responsibility indeed, including when not physically present. But at the same time, it is taken on without any complaint whatsoever. This is a small price to pay, if you even call it that, for the unflinching loyalty and unquestioning obedience that you get from them in return, even to the peril of their deaths.

So there it was – As a newly-minted 2iC, I was commanding the entire battalion on behalf of my Commanding Officer for the first time. By the way, if the code word for a commanding officer is *Tiger*, that for the 2iC is the stark opposite – *Lamb* is what he is called!

Feel free to make of it what you will!

However, it was a great learning opportunity indeed, especially since Col Chandran did not breathe down my neck, trying to find out what exactly was going on in the battalion from minute to minute. Instead, I made it a habit to call him once every 2-3 days to keep him updated as also seek his advice and guidance whenever needed. It worked fine for him too, since he was able to enjoy his vacation that much more!

This duration also helped me meet, measure, and bond with a bunch of youngsters who had been commissioned as officers into the battalion in my absence.

Young officers epitomize the spirit of any battalion anywhere in the Indian Army, be it in peace or even in field. They are the ones who are the most visible face of a battalion, since by virtue of their seniority, or lack of it, it is they who get tasked the most!

In my absence, the battalion had welcomed six new youngsters into its fold, each boasting a different personality. With the festival of Holi falling during the time I officiated, it was a great opportunity to know each one of them individually as well as collectively, both in professional as well as social settings. Of course, they too got to size me up, as did the rest of the men of the battalion, many of whom too were seeing me for the first time. And Holi was just the perfect occasion to do so.

Needless to say, the day was a riot of colours and a bit more!

The most important fact, however, was that we spent

the entire day together, first with the entire Battalion in the PT ground and later, amongst ourselves in the Officers' Mess, with the ladies and kids joining us. Old bonds were re-affirmed while newer ones were formed with the latest bunch of youngsters who were to form the *cutting edge* during my command.

As I have mentioned before, it was a homecoming indeed ... albeit, to a bunch of new family members, so to say.

All in all, the days flew by as I got re-acquainted with the Battalion as not just the 2iC, but the next *Tiger!*

Pretty soon, we got the news that Col Chandran had been nominated for the prestigious Higher Command Course. This put his latest date of departure sometime in the first half of June. With a short leave that he planned to apply for before departure, I was told by him to be mentally prepared to take over command of the Battalion by mid-May at the latest.

Alas, his plans for leave went haywire when the *'powers that be'* told him that they intended to keep him in the chair for as long as they could since he would be handing over the reins of the Battalion to a Lieutenant Colonel instead of a Colonel ranked officer as would normally be the case!

The Selection Board from Lieutenant Colonel to Colonel in the case of my batch was facing delays due to some reasons as I mentioned earlier. Hence, as per the interim solution promulgated by the organization, wherever absolutely necessary, Lieutenant Colonels would take over as *Officiating Commanding Officers,* and wherever they could, current COs would continue commanding till the time the selection board for their relievers was held.

So here I was, all set to take over the *Hot Seat* on 09 June 2016. The only catch was that I wouldn't be a Commanding Officer, but instead an *Officiating* Commanding Officer.

Now technically, it didn't make much of a difference because the orders that were issued in advance catered for empowering me with all the legal powers that a full-fledged Commanding Officer of the Indian Army was entrusted with.

However, I had my own doubts of a different kind altogether, as did some of my peers in a similar situation.

Technically speaking, we still hadn't been through the Selection Board for our next rank and quite appropriately, were only being appointed as Officiating Commanding Officers in our current rank of Lieutenant Colonel, instead of the rank of Colonel that Commanding Officers don in the Indian Army.

This led to a moral dilemma (*which I later realized, was of my own making!*) of how should I discharge my duties.

I would still be a Lieutenant Colonel and officially, merely an Officiating CO, even though I was empowered with all the requisite legal powers that came with the chair. To top it, there was no indicator as to when our Selection Board might take place and knowing the trends of the past, more than half of our batch would *not* make the cut, which might include me as well!

The dilemma was quite real and kept me occupied right up to a day prior to when I was to formally take over the reins of the Battalion from Col Chandran.

However, call it divine intervention or an epiphany, but

I finally found an answer shortly before the formal handing-taking over ceremony.

Here's the thought that brought about that much needed clarity:

A battalion needs a Commanding Officer to function normally, not an Officiating one!

Basically, I would sum it up as an organization needing a figure of authority not only to guide and lead it and be unabashed in utilizing that authority to set things right whenever needed, but also be one that is *seen* as such, i.e., a figure of authority.

Without this, the organization will merely be a headless body.

Thus, regardless of my official status, to the boys in the Battalion I would be their Commanding Officer. Period.

And this is exactly what I did – I decided to be the *Tiger*, and I proceeded to command my Battalion regardless of my official or for that matter, *officiating* status!

Not just that, pretty soon my higher headquarters too were used to me introducing myself as the CO and not as the officiating incumbent.

What I shall write next in this book (the original purpose of the book, in fact!) is about my journey as the *Tiger* of one of the most decorated Battalions of the Indian Army, about the mistakes I made, and about the lessons I learnt which might find resonance with those within and outside the profession of arms as well.

2

Settling Down

Leadership is not about being in charge.
Leadership is about taking care of those in your charge.

—**Simon Sinek**

The moment I took command and sat in the *Tiger's* chair for the first time was one of immense euphoria. It was a lifelong dream come true – commanding my own Battalion!

Of course, once the euphoria subsided (rather quickly, I'd say!), the next emotion was one of being overwhelmed at the sheer magnitude of the responsibilities that now lay on my shoulders!

Panic wouldn't be a wrong word to describe it!

What suddenly dawned on me was the fact that now there was no one else to take responsibility for whatever happened in the Battalion – good or bad!

There would be no more looking up to the *Tiger* for seeking a decision and then faithfully implementing it to the best of one's abilities without the burden of any judgment regarding the correctness of the decision or otherwise.

Col Chandran was in Station for just one day after handing over before he moved out. Even in those 24 hours, his mere physical presence was sort of a moral support.

But I hardly realized this till the moment he was finally seen off after a cup of tea in the Officers' Mess.

It was slowly sinking in!

The only parallel I can draw is that of holding my first child. Initially, it was sheer pride and excitement. Then, when he was three days old, it suddenly dawned on me that whatever he became in life would be a reflection of how good or bad a parent I was! And just like that, there was a momentary rush of panic before the sheer responsibilities of parenting took over!

By the way, the story of my elder child finds a partial mention later in this book in the chapter titled '*What Goes Around, Comes Around*'!

While parting, Col Chandran had offered his only advice to deal with what lay ahead. *'Just remember one thing. Have a large heart'*, was all he said. With the benefit of hindsight, I feel that was the only advice needed by me as a new *Tiger*, one that I too later passed on to my successor as well as to any officers about to assume command of their battalions.

So there was nothing much to do except to get on with the job of commanding the Battalion. To be fair, having a set routine and the daily grind did put the bout of initial panic to rest. Of course, having an excellent Brigade Commander and fellow Commanding Officers who gave me time as well as guidance to settle in my role helped as well.

But there was yet another facet of being a *Tiger* that had me sitting uneasy in the chair for the first few days.

It was peculiar to my Battalion.

As I mentioned earlier, mine is one of the very few Battalions of the Indian Army that have been conferred with the title 'Bravest of the Brave'. It is given to a Battalion/ Regiment that has earned two of the highest gallantry awards that the Nation bestows during war and peacetime – the Param Vir Chakra and the Ashok Chakra.

My Battalion earned an Ashok Chakra in 1997, thanks to the supreme sacrifice of 2nd Lieutenant Puneet Nath Datt in the Kashmir Valley and two years later a Param Vir Chakra in the 1999 Kargil War, courtesy Captain Manoj Kumar Pandey whose story also is well known.

Once again, I'll talk more in detail about this later in the book in the chapter titled *'Inherited Glory'*. But right now, here, I will talk about the larger-than-life presence of these two exceptional soldiers in my new office!

Befittingly, one of my predecessors had got portraits of 2nd Lt Puneet Nath Datt and Capt Manoj Kumar Pandey painted professionally. They occupied the pride of place in the *Tiger's* office. In my case, these two were put up on the wall right in front of my chair.

Hats off indeed to the artist who painted these very life-like portraits, but there was a flip side to it as well. It took me nearly two weeks to get used to the intense, unblinking gaze that they cast over me while I sat in the chair!

It was almost as if they were overseeing whatever the current incumbent was up to. I'll be wrong if I said that it wasn't unnerving in the initial days even though one did get used to their unending scrutiny after a while.

However, at the back of my mind I always knew that the standards set by the supreme sacrifices of these two fellow officers were sacrosanct and it was my bounden duty to ensure that they were not let down.

Needless to say, I slowly settled in my new appointment and went about in my own bumbling ways to command a body of nearly 800 fighting men in peace as well as in field conditions, never losing sight of the holy responsibility entrusted to me as a *Tiger*.

This, folks, is the story of how I settled into my new role as the *Tiger* of *First Battalion The Eleventh Gorkha Rifles (Bravest of the Brave)*. What follows in this book is an anecdotal story of my days in command, the mistakes I made, and the lessons I learnt.

--*

2Lt Puneet Nath Datt and Capt Manoj Kumar Pandey
Their Unblinking Gaze was a Constant Companion in my Office

CITATION

2nd Lieutanant Puneet Nath Datt, Ashok Chakra (Posthumous)

On 20 July 1997, Second Lieutenant Puneet Nath Datt was ordered to lead his company in the search operation. An information was received that a group of mercenaries were holed up in a house. 2/Lt Datt decided to begin the search from a suspicious-looking three-storeyed house that provoked the militants to fire back.

In a three hour long encounter, the fearless young officer kept taking pot-shots at the windows and lobbing hand grenades into the solidly-built house. 2/Lt Datt insisted on taking up the task of clearing the resistance.The moment he jumped over the wall of the house, he ran into a militant trying to make a dash for freedom and shot him dead. Thereafter, 2/Lt Datt kept on lobbing grenades at the first floor from where the last surviving militant was continuously firing. The militant spotted 2/Lt Datt and fired at him but at that very moment, 2/Lt Datt too spotted him and let off a burst that killed the militant. 2/Lt Datt sustained grave injuries and was evacuated to the hospital. 2/Lt Puneet Nath Datt displayed courage and valour of the highest order and laid down his life for the country.

For this valiant and courageous act, 2/Lt Puneet Nath Datt was awarded the Ashoka Chakra posthumously.

CITATION

Captain Manoj Kumar Pandey, Param Vir Chakra (Posthumous)

Lieutenant Manoj Kumar Pandey, a young officer of the 1/ 11 Gorkha Rifles, took part in a series of boldly led attacks during Operation Vijay, forcing back the intruders with heavy losses in Batalik, including the capture of Jubar Top.

His finest hour was during the advance to Khalubar, when he was Number 5 Platoon Commander. On the night of 2/3 July 1999, as the platoon approached its final objective, it came under heavy and intense enemy fire from the surrounding heights. The officer was tasked to clear the interfering enemy positions, so as to prevent his battalion from getting daylighted, being in a vulnerable position. The officer quickly moved his platoon to an advantageous position under intense enemy fire and sent one section to clear the enemy positions from the right, while he himself proceeded to clear four other enemy positions on the left. Fearlessly assaulting the first enemy position, he killed two enemy personnel and proceeded to assault the second and destroyed it by killing two more enemy personnel. Lieutenant Manoj Kumar Pandey was injured on the shoulder and legs by enemy fire while clearing the third position. Undaunted and without caring for his grievous injury, he led the assault on the fourth position urging his men and destroyed the same with a grenade, even as he got a fatal Medium Machine Gun burst on his forehead. It is this singular daredevil act of the officer, which provided the critical firm base for the companies, which finally led to capture of Khalubar.

Lieutenant Manoj Kumar Pandey, thus showed most

conspicuous bravery, indomitable courage, exemplary personal valour, outstanding leadership and devotion to duty of an exceptionally high order, in the face of the enemy and made the supreme sacrifice in the highest traditions of the Army.

Note: He is listed as a Lieutenant in the official citation because he completed the minimum qualifying service duration to be promoted to the rank of a Captain while in the middle of the Kargil War. Official orders to that effect couldn't be published due to the Battalion being in war. He sacrificed his life before the orders could be published and hence, the documentation carries the rank of Lieutenant.

--*

During my first tenure as a staff officer, I had come to realize that I needed some sort of distractions in my office in order to keep me focussed on the work at hand.

Yes, I know it is a rather ironical statement that I have just made, but that's just how I work!

So I would always have a television in my office that was tuned in to some music channel at low volume. This way, even if I lost focus from the work at hand, a few moments spent staring at the idiot box would be sufficient to get the mind back to where it was needed to be.

This habit continued for more than half a decade before I decided to switch over to a news channel instead of music during my Command tenure.

What triggered this was not a sudden distaste for music, or new-found love for current affairs.

Instead, it happened when I realized that the only photograph of the only occasion when my first Brigade Commander during my Arunachal Pradesh tenure came to my office was photo-bombed by Mrs. Twinkle Khanna!

3

REACHING OUT

If you knew how quickly people forget the dead,
You would stop living to impress people.

—**Christopher Walken**

This is a story that was nearly 17 years in the making. A story of how the battalion was finally able to re-establish a long lost association with the family of a long lost brother, that too while stationed at a remote and obscure corner of the Motherland.

Here is how it went...

From the very first days post my commissioning, as I learnt the glorious history of my Battalion, one name continued to stick with me all through my career, even as I learnt the ropes and added more and more years of newer and newer experiences in this journey of mine in the profession of arms.

It was the name of a young officer that we had lost during Operation Pawan in Sri Lanka. Now, for a Battalion raised just over a decade after independence, having lost quite many men in various operations was hardly a matter of surprise. But in this case, somehow this one name was always there at the back of my mind.

Let me tell you why.

Even though I joined the battalion barely 12½ years after we had lost him, I found hardly a couple of officers from that time who were still in the battalion. Consequently, his name or his story was rarely mentioned. Some of the senior NCOs and JCOs would still talk about him occasionally, whenever conversations ventured towards their days in battle in Sri Lanka.

What I knew was that he had been lost in an ambush.

But despite the occasional gentle prodding to those who knew, there wasn't often much more that was forthcoming.

Now don't get me wrong. After over almost a quarter century in uniform, I have come to realize that people do tend move on after a loss fairly quickly.

Yes, I am aware the above statement might come across as somewhat cold, for the want of a better word. So allow me to elaborate upon it.

With the likelihood of mortal injury being an ever-present reality, especially when deployed in field conditions or even in peacetime when handling live ammunition and explosives, I have seen soldiers, myself included, mourning lost comrades and then moving on fairly quickly, at least as a group. Individually, all lost comrades are missed by practically everyone who knew them, but as a group, soldiers do tend to move on so that they can go on to carry on fighting whenever duty calls, without any emotions holding them back. In fact, even in routine peacetime activities it is quite apparent – with postings lasting barely 2-3 years in the case of most officers, even the seemingly most indispensable ones are hardly missed once the next incumbent takes their place even if he has to start from the scratch!

Now back to this particular person that I just couldn't let go of.

The biggest reason was that hardly anyone talked about him.

Before you get me wrong, let me offer a disclaimer right here – all men lost in the line of duty had their names etched in the Battalion Quarter Guard, including the one I am talking about. However, to have lost an officer (one of only five that we have lost in operations thus far), and not even having a photograph of him was something that always bothered me.

Yes, the battalion had not only lost an officer, but also somehow lost many of the memories associated with him.

To be fair, one can't really blame anyone for this. From 1987, when the Battalion moved from Jaipur to Madras for further induction to Sri Lanka, it found itself almost continuously in operations all the way up to Operation

Vijay in 1999. In this duration, there were hardly two years in peace stations, that too with intermittent operational deployments thrown in.

In this duration, by the way, the battalion went on to earn a solid reputation for itself, earning a Param Vir Chakra as well as an Ashok Chakra within a span of less than two years between 1997 and 1999!

So naturally, in the midst of practically a decade-plus of near-continuous operations, certain other, equally important aspects did get overlooked.

Such was the case with the memory of 2nd Lieutenant Ramesh Rawat, who had given up his life somewhere near Batticaloa, Sri Lanka, on 6 June 1989. I first heard about him almost as soon as I joined the battalion in December 2001. But apart from the fact that he had died in an ambush, there wasn't much information that we had.

All through my years in service, this thing kept bugging me.

Ultimately, I did get my chance to make things right sometime within my first year in command of the battalion.

Somehow, all things just happened to fall into place to make this possible, almost as if some higher power had decided that it was time.

On a whim, I decided to try and find out whether the Indian Military Academy (IMA) had any personal details about him in their records. As luck would have it, one of the officers from my own unit, Prabhat, who was at that time posted as an instructor there, got on the job right away.

God bless the record keepers at IMA, for not only did

they still have the three-decade old file containing his residential address, but also able to guide Prabhat to it!

2nd Lt Ramesh Rawat had belonged to Pauri District in Garhwal, apparently.

The next task was to have someone go there physically and enquire about his family. Too bad, none of my officers or for that matter, Gorkha troops hailed from that part of the Motherland.

Looking back, it seems that it was for just such a contingency that the Almighty had ensured that my neighbouring battalion in Arunachal Pradesh at that time would be a Garhwal Rifles battalion!

One of my senior company commanders at that time, Satish, got in touch with his counterpart in the Garhwal Rifles battalion next door who pretty soon found one of his Garhwali boys on leave, not very far from the address that I wanted checked out. Unsurprisingly, two days later I had the mobile phone number of the father of 2nd Lt Ramesh Rawat.

Now, with the contact details of his father in hand, you would say that I rushed to call him up, right?

Well, it didn't turn out that way.

The wait to know a bit more about him was finally on the verge of conclusion, and I developed cold feet. I suddenly found myself full of doubts, contemplating whether to call him up or not.

Here's why I was suddenly unsure.

In my last 17 years of commissioned service, I was pretty sure that the Battalion had had absolutely no contact with his family. He had been lost in battle another 12 years before that, and I was reasonably sure that the Battalion had lost contact with his family not very long after his death in battle.

Now, when we were planning to get back in touch with the family nearly three decades later, I wasn't quite sure how they would react.

After a couple of weeks of mulling over it, I decided that instead of calling up myself, I'd request my 2iC to do so. The reason, at least in my mind, was that we would have a buffer between the family and the office of the Commanding Officer, in case the conversation was a bit less than friendly, so to say.

In the end, thankfully, it wasn't the case.

Yet another reason why I wanted my 2iC to initiate contact was that he was quite a mature person, with enough years behind him in service as well. I could, and indeed did, rely upon him to take care of a lot of tricky situations during the time he served as my 2iC.

So the 2iC, Vikas, made the call one fine morning.

The report that Vikas gave me was very encouraging. Apparently, the father of 2nd Lt Ramesh Rawat, who answered the phone, was pleasantly surprised and in fact, happy to hear from the Battalion. He made it a point to mention that he was happy that even after so many years, the Battalion hadn't forgotten them and had sought to contact them.

In another quirk of fate, we found that he was currently settled in NOIDA. It was not very far from my own home in New Delhi and pretty soon a plan was taking shape in my mind to go and meet them in person during my next leave which was just a couple of weeks ahead.

I still didn't call him up.

I still didn't know what to say to him.

This was also one of the unsaid reasons why I had requested Vikas to initiate the contact.

But that was to change soon. I left for Delhi on a short leave as earlier planned and dialled the number of his father the moment I reached home. Unlike in the case of Vikas, my talk with him was a bit formal and also short. I was still not very sure what to say to him. So I just took his home address and sought a suitable time to visit.

Two days later, I was headed to their residence in a taxi. Thankfully, I had brought a memento from the Battalion to hand over to them.

The doorbell was answered by 2nd Lt Ramesh Rawat's father, Honorary Flight Lieutenant Narain Singh Rawat, IAF (retired). Even in his old age, his bearing and body language were indicative of his own career as a soldier in the Air Force. The lady of the house met me soon thereafter and offered me a glass of water.

The conversation was a bit awkward in the beginning.

Then, about five minutes later, the younger son of the couple, Mahesh, joined us, presumably having taken half a day off from his job.

I repeated my story of seeking to know more about their son that had landed me there at their residence after a journey of 17 years. They too had their own stories to tell. Quite a few tears were shed as well that afternoon. All said and done, as the afternoon progressed, I could feel a weight lift from my heart – a weight I hadn't known that I had been carrying within me for so long.

The family told that one of the Battalion officers had come to their home sometime in 1990 after de-inducting from Operation Pawan. Sadly, that had been the last communication from the Battalion or anyone associated with it, till the time Vikas had ended up calling them up some weeks ago.

I was later told by Mahesh Bhaiya (the younger brother of 2nd Lt Ramesh) that his father had called him up as soon as Vikas had disconnected after that first call. He too was unsure what to make of that totally unexpected call which had come out of the blue. Mahesh Bhaiya and his father then decided to see how things went and thus, there I was, sitting in their home.

My hosts insisted that I stay for lunch and I couldn't refuse. As I departed, I had with me a photograph of 2nd Lt Ramesh Rawat, since sadly, we didn't have one in the Battalion.

That photograph was converted into two portraits by an NCO from the 'Charlie' Company, Rakesh, who was an exceptionally gifted artist. Today one portrait proudly adorns the entrance of the Officers' Mess, while the other was presented to the family on behalf of the Battalion by Major Rishabh of my Battalion who was posted in Delhi at that time.

Just under a year later, Mahesh Bhaiya and his wife visited us in Arunachal Pradesh, three days after the 29th anniversary of the loss 2nd Lt Ramesh Rawat. The annual 'Mandir Parade' on the death anniversary of each and every martyr of the Battalion that we had initiated some years ago, was delayed by three days in this instance so that his family members could also attend.

After the 'Mandir Parade' in remembrance of his brother, Mahesh Bhaiya spoke with the troops over a cup of tea. One could make out that he was quite overwhelmed with emotions and indeed, there were quite a few moist eyes all around pretty soon, as he spoke.

We hosted him for a couple of days as he and his wife went on an excursion to Tawang and thereabouts, before heading back to Delhi.

All in all, it was one of the most satisfying duties that I was fortunate to be the one to fulfil as the Commanding Officer of *'THE FIRST'*. I am glad to report that the association stays strong as ever and that 2nd Lt Ramesh Rawat's family were special invitees to the Diamond Jubilee celebrations of the battalion in a peace station not too long ago.

On a personal note, as I have mentioned above, it was nothing short of 'Mission Accomplished'.

In another twist of irony, 2nd Lt Ramesh's father told me when I first met him that he had actually written to the Army HQ as well as the Battalion regarding some problem with the pension of his late son, just about six months before Vikas called him up. He was actually under the impression that Vikas calling him up was a result of that. However, somehow that communication had never reached us. But as it turned out eventually, we too were actively looking to get in touch with him at about the same time, though for different reasons.

The pension issue was soon resolved, with some push from the Battalion.

It seemed that destiny was indeed nudging us towards re-establishing a long lost association. There were doubts as well within me and, as I later found out, within his family too. Yet, in the end destiny prevailed and any doubts were quickly cast aside as both sides got to know each other.

What did we achieve by all this? some might ask.

Well, my reply would be that in material terms, absolutely nothing whatsoever. Things would have continued as they were even if the Battalion continued to be out of touch with the family of one of its own officers lost in a war.

But what we gained was something far more valuable, yet unquantifiable. We brought yet another family *back* into the fold of the Battalion. Mind you, I use the word *'back'* because they had actually been a part of us while their son was alive, only for us to move on and lose touch due to various reasons.

What we also got was a face to associate with the memories, where earlier we only had a name, thanks to the magic woven by Rakesh and his paintbrush. What we gained, or rather regained, was yet another hero who now inspires the newest generation of soldiers of the Battalion.

As for what the family themselves gained, I can only offer what I have been able to perceive.

To be fair, nothing can ever compensate a parent for the loss of a child, or for that matter, a sibling who lost his elder brother, that too in the prime of his youth. That said, having known them for a little over four years now, I do get a feeling that stories and emotions that were tucked away in some dark corner of their hearts are gradually coming out. Colleagues that had no clue about the loss suffered by Mahesh Bhaiya do so now, thanks to his sharing a bit more about his brother all over again.

I wouldn't go so far as to say that they have found a closure since it is a loss that can never be forgotten, or made up. But I do get the feeling that with the Battalion back in touch with them, there is at least some solace that his sacrifice was not forgotten and will *never* be forgotten. And I get a feeling that he is mentioned in their conversations a bit more often than before.

In another twist of irony, I actually came across the quote mentioned in the beginning of this story when I was about halfway through writing it. It just seemed so apt, that using it in this story was a decision that was made instantaneously.

So, this is the story how 2nd Lt Ramesh Rawat finally came back into the family of 'THE FIRST' after nearly three decades.

On a personal note, my *second book – The India-Pakistan 'Tango' – ended up being dedicated to 2nd Lt Ramesh Rawat.*[1]

1. Kohli, Harpreet Singh. "*The India-Pakistan Tango*", Blue Hill Publishers.

Mahesh Bhaiya at the Battalion Location – 09 June 2018

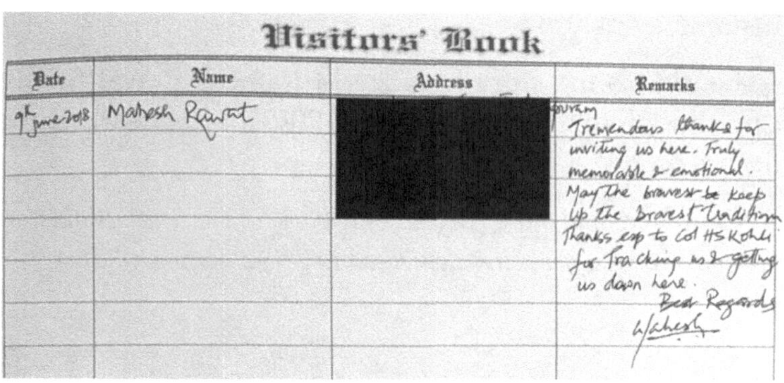

Visitors' Book

Date	Name	Address	Remarks
9th June 2018	Mahesh Rawat	[illegible]	Tremendous thanks for inviting us here. Truly memorable & emotional. May the bravest be keep up the bravest tradition. Thanks esp to Col HS Kohli for tracking us & getting us down here. Best Regards Mahesh

Remarks in the Visitors' Book After Lunch

At the Mandir Parade in Memory of his Brother

With the Men of the Battalion over a Cup of Tea after Mandir Parade

Mahesh Bhaiya at the Diamond Jubilee Celebration, seated next to Capt Manoj Kumar Pandey's Father and 2nd Lt Puneet Nath Datt's Mother

--*

It so happened that my Battalion was entrusted to run a small eatery by the highway that lay near the Brigade Headquarters location because we lay astride a popular tourist route, but one which didn't have many amenities for travellers due to lack of development in that region at that time.

Now this was yet another entity that functioned outside the Battalion location, and as such, mandated regular visits by Duty NCO/Duty JCO and even the Regimental Police NCO just to ensure that not only were things running smoothly, but that the boys running the shop were well turned-out as is expected of any soldier.

Every Saturday there used to be a gathering of all officers at the Brigade Headquarters to participate in a weekly seminar organised by the Division via video conferencing. This would give me a unique opportunity to ensure that I and all the officers would have our lunch at the eatery being run by our boys.

This was my preferred way of keeping an eye on things out there as well!

Anyhow, one fine Saturday I was pleasantly surprised to see 'You are under CCTV Surveillance.'

Needless to say, I was mighty impressed. Brigade Headquarters seemed to have pulled a surprise on us by their generosity, it seemed.

So I called the NCO in-charge and asked him to show me the CCTV cameras.

With a sheepish grin, he promptly replied that there were none!

Confused, I then pointed to the CCTV surveillance signs posted everywhere.

That NCO continued grinning and said that he had decided

to put them up after a set of salt and pepper dispensers had gone missing a couple of days earlier. Not only that, but he also proudly reported that ever since those signs went up, there had been no losses whatsoever!

All that I could do was grin along and compliment him on a job well done!

4

What Goes Around Comes Around!

"By each crime and every kindness, we birth our future."

—David Mitchell

This is a tale of serendipity, if I may call it thus. A tale of a gesture born out of an impulsive decision, which got paid back handsomely not very long thereafter.

As I mentioned earlier, the only advice which my predecessor gave me was to have a large heart. Over time, as I matured as a Commanding Officer, I realized that this was perhaps the only advice that was actually needed, especially with an exceptional team of officers and men that always put their best foot forward, come what may. All that they needed was a guy at the top who could guide and channelize their efforts, and give a pat on the back every once in a while!

So, onward with the story.

But before moving ahead, let me put in a word about what we call the *Interview Parade* in a battalion. It involves the *Tiger* personally interviewing each individual going out of the battalion or coming back. This includes people proceeding on or coming back from leave, professional courses, temporary duties, etc, plus those proceeding on retirement.

The Interview Parade is a mighty formal affair, with every interviewee in his best uniform for a formal audience with the *Tiger*, who is flanked by the Adjutant and Subedar Major of the Battalion. This is their one chance to air any issues directly to the *Tiger* and be assured of a quick resolution, in case they don't feel their own channels of reporting are prompt enough, or fair enough in their opinion.

Airing of concerns or grievances is a rare occurrence due to established channels of reporting in a battalion; however, and most of the interactions during an Interview Parade pertain to soldiers giving their personal details and the reason they are leaving or coming back. In my case, this was sometimes followed up with me asking some questions, or giving them a word of encouragement.

Thus, that day in October 2018 too wasn't much different when I came across a young Rifleman by the name of Akash Rai whom I hadn't seen before in the battalion. I remember noting that he didn't seem very cheerful either.

Anyhow, he introduced himself, giving out his army number, rank, name, etc. I realized he had put in about three years of service, yet I was puzzled why I hadn't seen him before.

He next mentioned that he had just been sent back to the unit by the Regimental Centre.

Ah, this makes sense, I silently mused, even as I wondered why such a young lad had been sent to the Regimental Centre in the first place.

So I asked him.

He replied that instead of sending him to the Battalion

after completion of his basic military training, he was retained with the Regimental Centre and attached with the 10m Air Rifle Shooting Team since he was a good shooter. He had trained with the team for nearly three years before he was despatched back to the Unit due to a recent dip in performance.

Thinking nothing much of it, I welcomed him to the Unit and told him to make himself useful in his platoon and get on with whatever task they were currently busy with.

With this, I moved on to the next person in the Interview Parade.

I was on the second individual after Akash when something suddenly made me turn my head towards him, and for the first and only time in my entire command tenure, I addressed a person whom I had already interviewed for the second time, while standing in front of another one.

I would normally call such individuals to my office after the end of the Interview Parade for a personal audience. But that morning, I just turned my head towards him and spoke to him again, even after his turn was over.

I asked Akash what weapon he had been using while at the Regimental Centre.

This young Rifleman replied that he had imported a rifle with his own money.

I had a fair idea of the cost of this sport and knew that even a basic rifle would have cost nothing less than Rs. 1,75,000. For a young lad to make such a purchase that would be worth at least five months' salary surely showed a commitment to the sport and, more importantly, confidence in himself.

And yet, here he was, sent back to the Unit because of a drop in performance. Given the fact that we were at that moment deployed in a far-flung part of the Himalayas, he stood no chance whatsoever to be able to pursue the sport for at least the next couple of years.

No wonder he wasn't in the best of the spirits that morning!

As a young lad quite low in the rung of the seniority ladder, he would have had no choice but to accept the orders that were given to him and leave a sport which he was good at and in which he had invested a sizeable chunk of his savings.

However, the next words out of my mouth changed this young guy's mood a bit, I think!

'I want you out of here tomorrow morning, heading back to the Regimental Centre to resume shooting', I told him, even as I noticed a subtle disapproval in the body language of the Subedar Major who might not have wanted to let go of a working hand in the battalion!

Regardless of the disapproving Subedar Major, Akash was smiling wide.

The next order went to the Adjutant to write to the Regimental Centre that we in the Battalion would bear the deficiency of a Rifleman for the duration that Akash was with them, training.

Of course, the Subedar Major was the next one to be tasked with ensuring that Akash moved post haste within 24 hours with the next available convoy!

Thus went Rifleman Akash Rai back to the Regimental Centre and the team that he had left hardly a couple of weeks earlier. A quick call to the Commandant of the Regimental Centre ensured that he was accepted back.

So finally, Akash was where he wanted to be, and to be frank, deserved to be. Meanwhile, life in the battalion went on as usual.

The next I heard from Akash was some time in December. He had called with a request related to his sport.

This time he wanted to move to New Delhi and be attached with a local unit there so that he could practise at the Dr. Karni Singh Range, which is one of the premier facilities for the sport in the country.

This too was accomplished after a few phone calls and our man Akash was soon training in Delhi.

Finally, his hard work paid off and he made his way into the national ranking system. This also meant he could now participate in qualifiers for international competitions which he did, and went on to compete successfully in a bunch of such competitions in India and abroad.

But then, this is not the reason why I chose to write this story here.

It so happened that my elder son too had just about started off in this very sport a few months before I found Akash standing in front of me in that Interview Parade. At that time my kid was just an amateur without his own kit, but once I realized he was not just good at it, but also keen to pursue the sport seriously, I finally bought him a rifle and rest of the kit sometime in April 2018.

As luck would have it, as my son improved and went on to train at the Dr. Karni Singh Range subsequently, Akash was right there to coach him as well, in addition to his regular coach!

Yup, life had indeed come a full circle and the *Law of Unintended Consequences* ended up returning the favour rather quickly.

To be fair, it wasn't really a favour I had done for Akash that day when I sent him back to the Regimental Centre, even if at the cost of the battalion making do with one rifleman less. All that I had done was to enable him to have another chance at succeeding at something that he was so passionate about.

And this, because I was uniquely in a position to do so, being the *Tiger* at that time!

Looking back, perhaps I understood it because my own son too was already taking his own first steps in the same sport. Maybe this was what led to the instantaneous decision to send Akash back to the Regimental Centre. But then, I couldn't have even in my wildest of dreams eve thought that this same lad would soon be helping my own child improve at the sport!

In the end, Akash went on to become a part of the Army Team, while my son too got into the national ranking system some time later and is still pursuing the sport with great vigour as I write this story, with Akash *Daju*[2] as well as some other members of the Services Team to coach and advise him whenever they run into each other!

---

2. *Daju* is the Nepali/Gorkhali way of addressing an elder brother. Kids of all officers in the Battalion address all riflemen and junior NCOs as *Daju*.

Of course, the joy on Akash's face that morning when I told him to go back to the Regimental Centre was enough feedback in itself to have told me that I had made the right decision!

Would you call it as I having a large heart as a Commanding Officer as was advised by my predecessor, or perhaps a quirk of fate precipitated by my own idiosyncrasy that morning, which ended up mighty fine for all concerned?

I shall leave that to your judgement.

I personally would see this as a lesson in empathy; a lesson in looking at the world from someone else's perspective; a lesson in utilizing your power and authority to help out someone who deserves another chance.

All that I'll say as I end this story is have faith in your people and in fate. Not only will they surprise you, but at times, will also end up doing you an unsolicited but solid favour!

An Interview Parade in the Hills

--*

Since the previous story starts with the 'Interview Parade', I thought it appropriate to tell another light-hearted one related to the same here.

The typical introduction that any interviewee gave of himself to the Commanding Officer was by giving out his Army Number, Rank, and Name, followed by the reason for he being in the Interview Parade that morning. This ended with the individual reporting, '.. aapke interview ke liye Hazir hai SHRIMAAN.'

The last 'SHRIMAAN' was shouted at the top of one's voice in order to signal the end of his report to the Commanding Officer.

The Interview Parade is always an very formal and serious affair, until one day when a nervous young soldier got caught in a twist of the tongue and ended his report to the CO with a resounding 'SHRI RAAM' instead of 'SHRIMAAN'!

Needless to say, the Interview Parade 'paused' for a while as folks tried to regain their composure!

5

Think Before You Speak!

"Speak when you are angry, and you will make the best speech you will ever regret."

—**Ambrose Bierce**

I'll start this chapter by quoting the late Uncle Ben of Peter Parker from the movie Spiderman, wherein he says '*With Great Power Comes Great Responsibility.*' I found this advice to be uniquely applicable during my time as the *Tiger* of my Battalion!

As a *Tiger,* the legal as well as financial powers that one is entrusted with are immense. However, more than that, in this story I intend to delve upon the *other* kind of power, that is, emotional, or moral, if you may call it that.

You see, the way the Indian Army generally functions means that Commanding Officers are placed on a pedestal merely by virtue of their rank and appointment. In fact, *It is Very Lonely at the Top* is quite an apt saying in this context. As my days in command progressed, I too gradually realized this fact and the immense responsibility that came with it.

As a Commanding Officer, any order given to the troops would be implemented to the 'T'. There might be some suggestions/discussions leading to the passing of an order. But once a decision was given, the entire team would put their best foot forward and ensure it got done in whatever form the *Tiger* wanted it because the ultimate responsibility/ accountability for the end result would rest with him and him alone!

As I have mentioned earlier, the buck truly stopped with the *Tiger*.

Then there was another part of being a *Tiger* that though known from before, took a while to get used to. It was the way your troops look up to you. Having grown up in the Battalion with them over the past so many years and earned their trust and respect, this was the only thing that was mine to lose in case I didn't live up to their expectations as their Commanding Officer.

Even to those outside the Battalion, be it the higher headquarters or sister battalions within the formation we were part of, it was the Commanding Officer who defined how a Battalion was perceived, either directly or indirectly.

I'll explain the above statement with an example.

When I was the Adjutant of the Battalion as a young Captain, the then *Tiger* had made it abundantly clear to me that saying 'yes' to any request by anyone was my privilege. However, in case any request was to be declined, it would only be after the CO said so.

Basically, what he ensured was that not only was the Battalion always willing to help out others, but that the normal bureaucratic delays of seeking his permission for such things were cut out. Yet, with barely three years of service behind me, I knew that this responsibility was delegated to me with full confidence in my own decision making capabilities by my CO. The unsaid part was that it would also be my decision whether or not to refer any such request to him in case I was doubtful about endorsing the same, or that it might be beyond our resources to oblige.

Yet, it was a continued lesson in magnanimity that my CO would hardly ever decline any requests referred to him by me, at times even to my chagrin. However, orders once passed were, of course, executed to the best of my abilities.

It was only after I myself became a CO that I gained a perspective into why he would do so. I found the reasons to be twofold.

Firstly, as the CO of an infantry battalion, the kind of manpower, and other resources at your disposal are quite substantial, especially when compared to other types of units or headquarters. Thus, it would be quite natural for them to lean on you once in a while.

Secondly (and more importantly!), as a *Tiger*, your job is not merely being a soldier, but also to a large extent, being a diplomat as well!

As I have mentioned earlier, a *Tiger* represents the Battalion to the world at large. Now before you get me wrong, I'll acknowledge that practically each and every soldier is a walking and talking representative of the Battalion to whosoever comes across them. But the role of a *Tiger* is much different.

He is the one who interacts most intimately with the senior officers up the chain of command on a daily basis. Hence, the need to be a diplomat, because perceptions of higher headquarters matter a lot when it comes to a lot of professional and even administrative matters related to a Battalion.

While things going wrong in-house can be managed by the *Tiger,* without anyone outside the Battalion needing to know, issues pertaining to outside entities have to be handled differently.

Thankfully, such instances are few and far between, and people are fundamentally good. However, in day-to-day dealings with higher headquarters, at times it is more prudent to just let some things pass!

So coming on to what this chapter is titled – *To Think Before You Speak*!

As I mentioned, the role of a Commanding Officer, or a *Tiger,* is pivotal to the functioning as well as reputation of a Battalion. Thus, each and every word you speak needs to be weighed before being spoken since the implications of a wrong order can be as bad as the loss of a precious life, or for that matter, a broken soul for getting shouted at for no fault of his.

Thankfully, in my case, such issues with higher headquarters or peer units were practically non-existent. In fact, looking back, I guess I was dealt a fairly good hand as far as people around me were concerned.

But as far as my functioning as the *Tiger* within my Battalion went, it took me a while to realize the value of holding my tongue so that I didn't end up saying something that I would regret later.

There were two reasons for doing so, as I learnt while in command.

Firstly, anything, especially a rebuke from a Commanding Officer, even if said in the heat of the moment was enough to spoil the day for any young soldier or even an officer. I am sad to say that in my case it happened more often than I would have preferred. Needless to say, I would almost always be overcome with guilt soon thereafter, but as some wise man once said, *words out of your mouth cannot ever be called back.*

Living with that guilt was the only penance I could do, knowing fully well that the person I had hurt by my words still wouldn't know of this.

In fact during my farewell address to the Battalion as I relinquished my Command, I started with an apology to all those whom I might have hurt by my words, knowingly or unknowingly. It was a small solace, but I just couldn't have left the Battalion without doing so.

A couple of stories stand out, which haunt me even to this day.

In the first instance, the son of a war-veteran of the Battalion was visiting Tawang on a personal trip. This meant that he would have driven past the Battalion location on his return trip. My 2iC got in touch with him to see if he could stop by for lunch or even a cup of tea. Alas, he was travelling by bus and couldn't.

So we decided to stop his bus by the Battalion location for a moment and give him a small token gift from the Battalion – a tie-pin with the regimental insignia. Accordingly, the Adjutant was tasked to get it packed. Now, just a little earlier, the 2iC had procured some new cards for packing these tie-pins when they needed to be gifted.

That morning I had to go to meet the Brigade Commander and decided that on my way out, I would see the new packing that was being talked about by the 2iC.

Unfortunately, the young rifleman entrusted with the packing didn't seem to have received the correct orders.

I still remember the scene.

On my way out, I stopped by the office of this young lad who came running to show me the gift he had packed. Unfortunately, it was the same old packing and not the new one.

Then I did something that I regret to this very day.

I lost my cool and admonished him.

All this because a small gift wasn't packed the way I expected it to be.

Even before I left the battalion, I knew that I had messed up by shouting at that youngster. He had merely done what he understood and, in fact, done a brilliant job of it. His only fault had been that he wasn't a mind-reader and didn't know what I had been expecting.

As for me, even as I type this story nearly five years after it happened, my heart is once again overwhelmed with guilt and grief all over again. This incident will haunt me till the day I die. I know this.

And all of it because I decided to talk before taking a moment to think with a cool head.

The second instance involved one of my young officers, Gaurav. He had been deployed on a forward post for a couple of months before being relieved by someone else and was happily on his way back to the Battalion Headquarters for a well-earned rest and recuperation.

It would be a three-day journey by convoy before he reached.

On the second day, the Adjutant told me that the Military Police have caught one of the unit personnel in that convoy with a little quantity of *Special Rations* (high calorie food items) authorised for troops deployed in high-altitude areas at the first staging area.

Now technically, the Military Police were correct in ensuring that rations authorised for high-altitude areas are consumed there itself. However, specifically in the case of my Battalion, with the Battalion Headquarters also located in a high altitude area, the troops were well within their right to carry such rations with them, unlike personnel of other battalions.

In fact, this is exactly what led to the matter being resolved, though not before a dozen or so phone calls had to be made over the next couple of days. In any case, all that he was found to be in 'illegal' possession of was a couple of chocolate bars and a packet of almonds!

Right in the middle of one such phone call, newly-promoted Captain Gaurav entered my office, all smiles!

And I let him have it for not ensuring that troops were aware of the orders!

Now here was a youngster, back in the Battalion Headquarters after a few months out in the middle of nowhere, and all he wanted that morning was to give a quick report to his CO. What he got in return was a bollocking for something that wasn't even his fault.

Yes, it was *my* fault that he got an unwarranted earful and that too after coming to my office for the first time in months.

A couple of years later, it was Gaurav himself who reminded me of this incident when he and his wife had come over to my place for a meal a few weeks after his marriage.

He hadn't forgotten.

And to be frank, neither had I.

We laughed it off that night over a drink at my expense, but such memories do tend to linger on for a really long time, as life has taught me over the four decades plus that I've been around.

In both these cases I could have just taken a few deep breaths before opening my mouth and these painful memories that are now so deeply etched in my heart, would just not exist. This applies equally for the young lad who packed those gifts, whose name now escapes me, as well as Gaurav, who too shall have the same memory, though from their perspective as the recipients of unwarranted admonishment.

The second reason why over time I realized that holding my tongue for a while was a good policy was that the initial input based on which you say something or give a decision/ order may not contain all the facts or even the correct facts.

It took me some time to realize this, of course at the cost of a snafu here and there!

Ultimately, I made it a personal policy to hold my thoughts to myself for at least 24 hours before saying anything or deciding anything on contentious issues, even if they ended up with me filled with rage.

Before proceeding ahead, let me put in a word for anyone who might have gotten the impression that I have anger issues!

Well, nothing could be farther from the truth, I'd say!

However, as a Tiger, anything and everything to do with the Battalion ultimately lands on your desk because it is, after all, your responsibility. And being emotionally attached to the Battalion which has indeed been a home away from home, even a minor issue that might end up with someone from outside getting a wrong impression of the Battalion does tend to rile one up.

This chapter is, in fact, due to me having learnt my lessons thanks to the mistakes I made!

So back to the story now.

What I realized was that in many cases, just delaying a decision by a day would help one get a much better perspective and a much better picture of the issue at hand, especially if it wasn't something that merited instant resolution.

There's one more example that I will share.

One fine evening I got a call from my Adjutant (*Yes, it's always the Adjutant!*) who told me that he had got an order from the Brigade GSO-1 regarding detailment of an officer for some task.

In the Adjutant's version, the GSO-1 had told him off a bit brusquely and suggested the name of another officer to be detailed.

Now this is something that is a strict no-no in my book!

It is specifically the Battalion's prerogative as to which officer is to be tasked for what detailment, unless the requirements are very specific. For a higher headquarters to specifically request for a particular officer by name for a detailment that could have been fulfilled by practically any other officer available at that time, was a bit odd.

So I picked up the phone and called up the GSO-1.

He answered the phone with a quick *'Good Evening, Sir'*, and the first words out of my mouth were *'Nitin, stop detailing my officers by name.'*

Yes, instead of trying to find out the other side of the story, I had chosen to tackle the issue with barely half the facts in hand!

Needless to say, I had to quickly eat my words as the correct perspective emerged. It was merely an issue of miscommunication and misinterpretation of orders!

A bottle of wine along with an apology was sent to the GSO-1 the next day!

This entire fracas could have easily been avoided had I waited a while and tried to find out the other side of the story as well. In fact, this very thing would have prevented at least a few more such embarrassing situations had I just waited a while.

Thankfully, I did learn this lesson at least partly as I grew in my command. More often than not, merely waiting for 24 hours before reacting would help in two ways. One, that I would be more rational and empathetic in my reaction; two, more facts or a clearer picture would automatically emerge without even the need to actively seek more information about the issue at hand.

Many a time, this would even mean that there was nothing that was needed to be done about the issue at all. And all of this, because I had chose to wait a bit!

Sadly, I would be wrong if I said that I was entirely successful in this endeavour. However, at the same time, looking back, I can also confidently say that I did learn the value of *aiming before shooting*.

I'll end this chapter by saying that when you are angry, it is not you who is in the driving seat; instead, it is your emotions that drive you.

Do take a moment to mull over what I have written above, before moving on!

--*

One fine day in the hills, sometime during the winter of 2018, I got a message that a former Commanding Officer would be visiting the Battalion by chopper the next morning. Understandably, quick orders were passed and the Battalion was soon preparing to receive and host him after a long gap!

All were happily awaiting his arrival .. well, all of us except one guy, the Subedar Major of the Battalion!

He came over to my office about an hour after the orders were passed, looking all confused and even a bit unsettled.

After the customary salutations, he blurted out, "Saab, General Saab aayenge kaise?" (Sir, how will the General come?)

Thinking that he may have missed the part about his mode of transport, I told him he would be coming by chopper.

The next question from the Subedar Major had me stumped again.

This time he asked, "But where will the helicopter land?"

All I could muster in reply was, 'Helipad', after taking a couple of moments to actually reconfirm mentally that the huge helipad which was about five minutes' drive from the Battalion location wasn't actually a figment of my imagination!

But he wasn't convinced.

The reason for that soon became apparent when he uttered the next words.

"Lekin Saab, kal helipad par toh hamara cricket match hai Maratha Battalion ke saath ..."

(But Sir, tomorrow we have a cricket match with the Maratha Battalion at the helipad.)

I am not kidding when I say that it took me all my will power to stop myself bursting out in laugher at the genuinely innocent query of the Subedar Major!

"The match will be rescheduled for the day after tomorrow," I said.

Case closed!

The Rescheduled Match was a Great Success!

--*

One day when I was away at the Division Headquarters for some work, I got an excited call from Shiv, my then Adjutant.

"SIR, WE ARE GETTING A MiG TOMORROW", he practically shouted in excitement over the phone!

But instead of sharing his excitement, I threw back a question at him.

"MiG?", I asked.

"YES SIR. TOMORROW", Shiv continued and further added that the Brigade GSO-1 had personally told him.

I merely told him to call up the Brigade GSO-1 again and confirm where the aircraft was to come. I had my doubts because such an exercise would normally be known at least a couple of weeks in advance.

About 10 minutes later, Shiv called up again and this time, with considerably lowered enthusiasm and even a hint of a doubt in his voice, reported that it would be landing at the local helipad near the Brigade Headquarters!

Now I realised what was happening, but instead of correcting him I decided to let him find out for himself. So I told him once again to call up the Brigade GSO-1 and ask him the purpose of the allotment.

This time he called back within five minutes and sheepishly told me that it was not a MiG but an Mi-17 helicopter sortie that had been allotted to the Battalion for routine training!

And this, folks, is the story of how Captain Shiv of the Indian Army found himself giving a PowerPoint presentation on the 'Aircraft of the Indian Air Force' to all officers of the Battalion the next weekend!

I am glad to report that he has never confused a helicopter for a fighter aircraft since that day!

Training Never Ceased, Come What May!

6

THE INVINCIBLE HUMAN SPIRIT

"If My Mind Can Conceive It and My Heart Can Believe It, Then I Know I Can Achieve It."

—Napoleon Hill

I wrote this story for my previous book, *'The Other Side of a Soldier'*. This is about a mutual interaction between me as a Commanding Officer and my Pipe Band, spread over almost the entire three-odd years of my command.

It was an interaction that ultimately turned out to be for the good of all concerned; an interaction wherein I cautiously pushed them more and more and they kept on delivering, at times surprising not just me but even themselves.

It was indeed an interaction that taught me how to be a good *Tiger* and taught the Band Platoon that there really were no limits to what the human mind can will the body to achieve.

It is a story worth retelling over and over again.

Hence my decision to share it in this book as well!

* * *

Mother Earth for sure has bestowed our Nation with an unparalleled bounty across its length and breadth.

However, as if to balance out this largesse, she has also ensured that most of the borders of the country are .. to put it very mildly .. '*challenging*' to man and defend.

However, there is no doubt that the Indian Armed Forces have risen to the occasion each and every time and ensured that difficulties of geography / climate are never an impediment when it comes to securing these borders against natural as well as other challenges thrown up by recalcitrant neighbours.

The Indian soldier is forever alert, right from the icy heights of the Siachen Glacier, down the difficult hills of the Line of Control with Pakistan and the Line of Actual Control with China, upto the deserts of Rajasthan, the never-ending Rann of Kutch and the rainforests of Arunachal Pradesh and other North-Eastern States.

One question that doesn't get asked often enough is – *What makes him do so?*

There are no easy answers to this question, except for the romantic phrase – *Human Spirit.*

Now, I am certainly not a poet who can write beautiful prose in describing this intangible quality that makes the Indian soldier what he is. Instead, what I will do is to share a couple of stories from my own experiences, with the hope that you, Dear Reader, will be able to get some sort of an understanding of what I cannot otherwise describe.

This one pertains to the Pipe Band of my battalion.

I came back to my Battalion after a nearly three year tenure as a staff officer in a brigade headquarter, followed by the Senior Command Course. The Battalion was located in a small town in semi-rural India at that point in time.

Soon after landing back, I took over the command of my Battalion, sometime in the month of June.

June was also the time of school vacations and with two young brats at home, I decided to organize a week-long 'Children's Summer Adventure Camp' at the Battalion level in order to keep all such kids of the battalion engaged during their vacation period.

The Camp duly commenced on a Monday and the kids got engaged. It was on Thursday that I decided to organize a concert by the Battalion Pipe Band for them as well, on the closing day that was less than 48 hours away.

Now before moving on, let me put in a word about the role of a Pipe Band in a battalion. I'll start by saying that a good Pipe Band enjoys the place of pride in an infantry battalion. It is mostly comprised of about 15-20 men who play military music using Bagpipes, Cymbals and various percussion instruments.

I sent for the NCO-in-Charge of the Pipe Band, Havaldar Suraj, and told him about my plan.

His reaction wasn't entirely surprising – He started sweating!

Part of the reason was that the time given to him was extremely short. I understood that. But the bigger reason, however, was that I knew that the Pipe Band had settled into a comfortable routine that involved showcasing their melodies while remaining static, without the need for any elaborate movements that I was now asking them to showcase. In fact, the last parade that they had participated in, had happened more than six years ago.

So here was Suraj, a talented 'Band Major', entrusted

with a bunch of equally talented musicians, all sweats inside my office!

But then, orders couldn't be refused, especially those pertaining to strictly professional requirements. So off went Suraj, with an assurance that this display was merely for the kids of our own battalion and within our own battalion lines. That was some consolation, in addition to the fact that the only parameter I gave him was to keep it to a minimum of 15 minutes. Beyond that, he was free to plan the display as he deemed fit.

He didn't know it then, but another reason was that I actually wanted to see the state of the current preparedness of the band. The short reaction time, though unintentional, only added to the challenge.

To cut a long story short, my Pipe Band put up a mesmerizing display for the Battalion's kids in the Battalion football field that morning, to everyone's amazement. This performance not only gave confidence to me, but also rekindled the confidence of the band-members themselves.

If only they knew what lay in store for them in the coming days and weeks!

Next Monday I called the entire Pipe Band to my office and after giving them a hearty 'Shabash' for the performance, I threw another challenge at them.

The Battalion's Battle Honour Day was three weeks away, and this being the last Battle Honour Day in the current station, I intended to celebrate it in the grandest possible manner. In addition, it would also be the first major event that I would be hosting after assuming command of the Unit. This time, I tasked the Pipe Band to put up a similar, 20 minute display in the Officers' Mess. Another thing that I told them was that I wanted to see the 'DHOLI', or the drummer, 'dance' during the drummers' display. This was something that the battalion's Pipe Band hadn't done for quite some time now. These two conditions apart, the band was free to decide upon how they wanted to choreograph their performance.

Entrusting the Battalion Adjutant to oversee their preparations, I got busy with my own work. I finally decided to see a rehearsal by Suraj and his boys three days before the main event.

I will be lying if I say I wasn't mightily impressed!

Left to plan it themselves, the boys had gone beyond my wildest expectations and all that I could offer was yet another pat on the back!

Needless to say, the event was a stunning success and well appreciated by all, with the band dishing out a full complement of Indian and English tunes. The capstone of the performance was two bagpipers walking in from both gates of the Mess, playing *Amazing Grace* as they approached the rest of their mates in the band who then joined in the symphony, ending it with a high.

Pats and compliments flowed thick and fast, right from the Division Commander down to the youngest of the subalterns who had witnessed the performance.

Naturally, Suraj was beaming with pride when I called him over to my office the next morning.

The entire band, as lined up outside my office, knew that they had done an excellent job and were looking forward to yet another pat on their backs by their Commanding Officer.

Of course they got that, plus two weeks of furlough.

And then they got yet another challenge thrown at them!

The Battalion's Raising Day was just about two months away. They were tasked to put up another performance at the same venue, with bulk of the same guests in attendance as well. This meant that they not only had to come up with a new routine, but it would also have to better their previous one, since nothing less would be acceptable to their *Tiger*!

Needless to say, they delivered yet another magical performance that night.

When they were called yet again to my office for more compliments, Suraj decided to come up with a personal request of his own. With barely two years to retirement, he wanted to get posted out of the Battalion in order to add on to his experience. He had already started training his replacement in anticipation.

This was a request that just couldn't be declined, thanks to his hard work in the band over the past many years, which was also the reason that he hadn't had an exposure outside of the Battalion. What further helped make that decision was the fact that the battalion was shortly to move to a field location where the Pipe Band wouldn't be called upon as often.

If only I knew how wrong I was!

Anyhow, I interviewed the next *Band Major* – Havaldar Subhandeep. He seemed a bit shaky at the prospect of assuming the responsibility that awaited him, especially in the wake of Suraj. At some level I too empathized with him.

But orders were orders!

So Suraj took Subhandeep under his wings and over the next six weeks, put him through the paces, before leaving the Battalion for good. Soon enough the battalion moved out for a field tenure in a cold and high altitude area. The new garrison of the battalion was located 12,000 feet above sea level.

The new location was hardly conducive for the Pipe Band to carry on its routine practices because of three major factors – high altitude leading to lack of adequate oxygen for the musicians playing wind instruments, extreme cold weather and its adverse effects on the bags of the bagpipes and lastly, lack of an open space of adequate dimensions to enable them to practice.

However, not too keen to let the band go out of practice, I sent them to another location situated at a relatively lower altitude, about six hours' drive away, to a battalion that was being commanded by a coursemate of mine. He not only took my band in, but also utilized them to train his own band as well. Together, the two bands participated in the Republic Day celebrations in his Division where his own boss was surprised to see my Battalion's Gorkhas perform!

When summers came, I got them back to the Battalion since I needed to maintain a certain minimum level of manpower at that location in those months. Once again, they kept practising whenever time permitted. The weather was relatively warmer, but still cold enough to necessitate devising of ways and means to keep the musical instruments safe. To that end, rum was used quite liberally to line up the innards of the bags of the bagpipes in order to prevent them from cracking and breaking up due to cold!

Needless to say, they were employed for ceremonial functions as well as Officers' Mess functions from time to time, while in the Battalion location. However, when the winters came yet again, they were ready to head down to their previous location for practising.

Only this time, I refused to grant them the permission to do so!

I had seen them practise in the high altitude Battalion location, outside of their comfort zone, and I had seen them adapt to it. In fact, within a few weeks of they coming back to the Battalion location, I had made up my mind that they were capable of not only practicing, but also performing at this altitude.

All that was left to be done now was to convince them that they indeed could do it!

There were long faces when they heard of this news, especially in the case of Subhandeep. His was a peculiar case, as I had come to realize. Having been in Suraj's shadow for so many years, he had some sort of inertia in him when it came to trying out something new because now delivering upon it would be solely his responsibility. But then, I had also realized that a little bit of push was all that he needed and once he got going, he would produce magic!

This *push* came in varied forms. Depending upon the

time and situation, it varied from gentle words of encouragement to outright summons followed by clear-cut orders.

In the end, the one thing that was a constant was his, and the rest of the band's talent for music. And they more than rose to the occasion each and every time, even at 12,000 feet above sea level!

However, in order to perform at such conditions, they inserted a unique drill in their routine – A one minute 'breathing break' after every 7-8 minutes. This was an absolute necessity in order to ensure that the band members stayed physically capable of finishing the performance.

They performed far and wide, even under the field conditions. Yet, the most memorable performance for me personally happened sometime in the month of April 2018 when my battalion's Pipe Band performed for all officers of the entire garrison at the lawns of the Brigade Commander's residence. It was a magnificent 26 minute performance amidst gusty winds and even a light drizzle in-between.

That Saturday morning, the hills and the valleys surrounding the Brigade Commander's residence reverberated with one melody after another dished by Subhandeep and his boys, of course with three 'breathing breaks' thrown in for good measure.

Later that year, on the occasion of the Dussehra festival in 2018, they put up another splendid, 24 minute long display for the entire battalion, along with a host of guests that had been invited to take part in the festivities. This was the highest altitude at which they performed a routine comprising elaborate movements and melodies.

It was also on this day that all my Pipe Band members were given an out-of-turn promotion in the form of local ranks by the Deputy Brigade Commander.

It was as much an acknowledgement of their talent as it was of the sheer hard work they had put in over the past 20 months or so, pushing themselves as well as their equipment to the limits, and then a bit more.

In the process, they had also ended up teaching *me* a LOT of lessons in human perseverance and leadership. Lessons, which hold good even today, nearly four years since I handed over the reins of the Battalion to my successor.

I shall remain forever indebted to Suraj, Subhandeep and their boys for what they taught me, even as they pushed themselves to the vey limits and beyond.

The Pipe Band under Havaldar Suraj, just before the performance for the kids in the Battalion Football Field

The Pipe Band under Havaldar Suraj performing for guests at the Officers' Mess on the Raising Day (Do note the dancing 'Dholi'!)

April 2018: The Pipe Band Performing under Havaldar Subhandeep at a High Altitude Location, Pushing Men and Instruments to the Very Limits

Subhandeep Leading yet another Pipe Band Display on a Foggy Morning in the Hills

--*

Col Rana was the Tiger of a Rashtriya Rifles Battalion deployed in the thick of operations in the Kashmir Valley. He knew that it was a stressful tenure for all his troops. However, professional commitments are non-negotiable and consequently, his men were quite busy with operations as well as routine security and administrative tasks.

Col Rana knew that this was something beyond his control. However, there was one thing that he could control – the leave of his men. Thus, as one of the biggest incentives that he could offer to his boys in return was a promise that each and every one of them would be able to avail their full 90 days quota of leave.

Mind you, this was a really bold decision indeed, since professional commitments demand a never-ending supply of working hands, more so in the area that he was deployed. But regardless, he went ahead and implemented his policy.

Needless to say, morale in the Battalion was high and it reflected in the operational successes they accumulated!

However, there was a caveat to his offer by the Tiger. What he asked in return was for his boys to rejoin from leave when due. Anyone overstaying was guaranteed an official disciplinary action. This ensured that his Battalion's manpower planning wasn't much disturbed.

Of course there were some defaulters and as promised, they were awarded the strictest of official punishments because not only had they disobeyed orders, but due to them, someone else would have had to reschedule his leave.

In the midst of this all came Sepoy Manohar, a driver posted to the Battalion, who had returned from leave a full 30 days late!

As promised, he was Marched-Up to the Tiger for his punishment.

However, during the disciplinary proceedings, Manohar made a plea to his Tiger. He had applied and was preparing for commissioning as an officer via the in-service commissioning route in the Army and an official disciplinary record in his profile would render him ineligible.

Here, Colonel Rana faced a moral dilemma.

The guy's plea had undisputed merit. However, he didn't want to make an exception for him for two reasons. Firstly, he would be going back on his word by not punishing this particular individual. And secondly, and more importantly, Manohar and Colonel Rana had served together in the same Rashtriya Rifles Battalion barely three years ago and any leniency to him would trigger rumours and loose talk about favouritism.

Yet, Tiger decided to let him off the hook instead of punishing him.

That was the first time he had done so.

Life continued as usual and soon Colonel Rana too handed over command of the Battalion to his successor and moved on.

Colonel Rana (who is now a Brigadier) still recalls with a smile the day he got a call out of the blue. It was Gentleman Cadet Manohar calling from the Indian Military Academy.

It took him a while to realize which Manohar he was speaking with!

Yes, the same Sepoy Manohar had made it through the rigorous selection process and was calling his former Tiger just before he was to be commissioned as an officer after completion of his training.

Here was a Tiger who had decided to trust his instincts and be large-hearted, even at the cost of going against his own policy and decided to give the young lad a chance. And that young lad had more than done his bit by making sure he succeeded. But what's more is that he hadn't forgotten that act of his Tiger who was well within his rights to have disregarded his plea and given him a well-deserved punishment that day. That was the reason he had hunted around to find out the current contact number of his Tiger before becoming an officer.

As far as Brigadier Rana goes, he has a wonderful and heart-warming story to tell to anyone interested!

7

TOUGH LOVE

Whoever imposes severe punishment becomes repulsive to the people;
While he who awards mild punishment becomes contemptible.
But whoever imposes punishment as deserved becomes respectable.

—**Chanakya**

The *Tiger's* role in a Battalion is something akin to that of a family elder – guiding and advising folks how to run the show. Trust amongst all of us, seniors, and juniors as well as peers is implicitly guaranteed, given the way Units of the Indian Army function.

Trust as well as empathy are absolutely vital for an entity that is the ultimate arbiter of any argument put forward by the Nation, one that is entrusted to enforce the Nation's *Will* on the battlefield.

Of course, this applies to leadership in any and every organization in practically every field that has human beings working for other human beings, but the stakes in the profession of arms are just a bit 'different'!

The challenge that one faces as the *Tiger* is to strike a good balance between benevolence as the head of the family and mission readiness of the Battalion. This is indeed a really thin rope on which one has to tread as a leader of men that are entrusted with putting their own lives on the line on his orders, should the Motherland require them to.

Also, like every other aspect of leadership, this too can be *taught* in a classroom/academic environment to only some degree. Ultimately, one learns on the job.

This story is about one of the 'problem boys' of the Battalion who needed fairly liberal doses of *Tough Love*; a story that saw *both* of us grow over the months and years that it shaped up.

This is the story about the journey of Naik Ratan.

It commenced almost as soon as I assumed command of my Battalion. So, in a way, it was also about me still being in the process of being judged by my troops in my new role as their *Tiger*. It would, in a way, set the tone about how I would be as a CO over the next few years. Of course, I say this with all the benefits of hindsight! At that point in time, I only did what I felt was the correct way of dealing with such things.

It so happened that within the first or second week of my command, I got a report from the Duty JCO that the night guard commander at the No. 2 Gate of the Battalion was found drunk during his nightly rounds.

Now this is a really big deal, especially for the commander of a guard that controls the main entry to the Battalion. Granted that the Battalion was serving in a peace station at that time and there wasn't any real threat due to a drunken NCO in charge of a guard, but principally it was a very serious situation because, such a thing repeating itself in an operationally active area could have really dire consequences indeed.

This was also the first disciplinary case brought to my knowledge as a CO.

The next order was quick. Ratan was to be marched up for a disciplinary hearing so that he could be punished commensurate with his rank and the offence that he had committed.

On the appointed day, the Subedar Major reported that Ratan had proceeded on Sick Report without informing his chain of command and was now admitted in the Military Hospital in the garrison.

This was a really interesting situation indeed!

I sent for his company commander and his senior JCO. What transpired was that Ratan had been a repeat offender, particularly due to his drinking habits. The Subedar Major also chipped in that on more than one occasion in the past, Ratan had proceeded on sick report when caught on the wrong side, including when summoned by the Subedar Major himself.

My next order was to put up his official disciplinary record to me.

For a guy that was described as a repeat offender, the official record was surprisingly mild. All he had to show for his repeated misdemeanours were two *Black Ink Entries* and one *Red Ink Entry,* that is, two reprimands and one severe reprimand!

I looked quizzically at the gathering in front of me and the senior JCO sheepishly replied on many occasions they would discipline Ratan within the Company by giving him field punishments or extra duties.

So this is what created the problem? I remarked to no one in general.

Of course, the folks in my office were studiously avoiding my gaze! The concept of field punishments and extra duties worked fine when he was a rifleman, but as an NCO, it was no longer an option.

But my remark or, for that matter, avoidance of eye contact by them still didn't quite solve the problem at hand.

After mulling over the entire fracas, I decided to call the Commandant of the Military Hospital to apprise him about his latest hospital admission and his background!

Thereafter, I told him that I will be sending him a *Form 10* for Ratan, a medical form for counselling.

In any case, Ratan did require psychological counselling. It might have actually helped him straighten his life had the same been done about a decade earlier when he first started becoming a nuisance. However, it was still a case of *better late than never.*

When Ratan was ultimately discharged from the hospital a couple of weeks later, I called him for formal counselling.

A formal counselling is different from a disciplinary march-up (which I had decided to forgo in this instance), in that it is more of an advisory interaction.

Ratan was told to sort himself out and start assuming the responsibilities that he is expected to shoulder by virtue of being an NCO.

There was another reason for this one-to-one interaction with Ratan that I chose. He and I had been part of the Battalion football team in 2003 and 2004 wherein we were unbeaten divisional champions for both years. So that factor too played up, though unsaid.

(The story of those football days is chronicled in my book 'The Other Side of a Soldier')[3]

The counselling by a trained psychiatrist seemed to have worked its magic on Ratan, who actually became a lot more responsive NCO. Either that, or it was the shock effect of having had a *Form 10* filled and a consequent hospital stay that lasted much longer than what he might otherwise have planned!

But the bottom-line was that he indeed seemed to have gotten his act together a bit and could be entrusted with responsibility without his seniors having to worry or to constantly keep him under supervision.

However, having been set in his ways for long, Ratan did slip up on more than one occasion.

But this time it was different.

For each and every disciplinary issue created by him, he was marched up to be officially punished.

A March-Up to the Commanding Officer and receiving a punishment served two purposes for any soldier who was at its receiving end. Firstly, it resulted in a permanent entry in the individual's service record; and secondly, a march-up was a matter of public knowledge and the

3. Kohli, Harpreet Singh. *"The Other Side of a Soldier"*, Blue Hill Publishers, p. 1.

embarrassment caused was a punishment in itself, especially if the recipient was someone relatively senior such as Ratan in this case.

Anyhow, over the course of the next 25-odd months, Ratan had accumulated one additional *Black Ink* and three additional *Red Ink* entries. With a total of four *Red Ink* entries, I was well within my legal rights to recommend termination of his service in the Indian Army.

This was known to Ratan as well.

In fact, another soldier from his own company had just been terminated from service by being given what is called a Local Discharge after my recommendation due to his disciplinary record. And this individual had to be let go even before he had completed the minimum service required to earn a pension. Thankfully, Ratan had completed the minimum qualifying military service for earning his pension.

After giving him his fourth *Red Ink* entry and he getting marched out as per the formal procedure, I called Ratan back to my office in the presence of his company commander and senior JCO as well as the Subedar Major.

This was to be yet another short counselling session.

As soon as he came in, I asked Ratan whether he wanted to carry on serving in the Battalion or whether I should recommend his discharge.

Though I didn't realize it at that point in time but today, with the benefit of hindsight, I think it finally clicked in Ratan's head that I was giving <u>him</u> the choice about what he wanted his future to be.

His reply was instantaneous.

He said he wanted to continue serving in the Battalion.

So I offered him yet another chance, this time making it clear that it was up to him to ensure how long he served.

This, I think, was yet another turning point because thereafter Ratan didn't give me any other occasion to punish him. It was immensely satisfying to see him finally rise to the responsibility expected of him as an NCO.

So much so that the Subedar Major made him in-charge of a snacks outlet that the Battalion was running for transient troops at the local Transit Camp. Here he was, after all those years of being a trouble child of the Battalion, now independently handling cash on behalf of the same Battalion while being away from direct supervision due to the physical distance between the Battalion Headquarters and the Transit Camp.

He couldn't get his next promotion, though, but ultimately completed his *Colour Service* and retired honourably.

Once again, at the end of it, all I'll say that both he and I had matured as individuals as well as a leader and the led. Somehow, for whatever reasons, I was willing to give him a chance to carry on serving, but only AFTER making it amply clear that it was to be a no-nonsense deal since one more slip-up and I would ensure that Ratan was thrown out of the Army.

In the end, I think this was all that was required to be done since his reply to my question after that final march-up was instantaneous and it was *that,* which was the turning point in his story.

One can only imagine the state of mind of that individual

with his disciplinary record in the dumps and enough for him to be sent on a local discharge at his *Tiger's* discretion. Then he is called back to the same office where he had been awarded his latest punishment, and is offered a final choice.

I am glad to report that *Tough Love* worked in this particular case, and dare I say, in at least a few more cases. I'm sure a few more potential *trouble kids* of the Battalion would have seen the possible consequences of breaching discipline and chose *not* to do so!

Let me end this particular story by addressing a question which some of you might have – Did he become a saint after being subject to this *Tough Love*?

Heck, no!

But then, who amongst us can say that for ourselves in any case?

I was satisfied with him merely becoming a better soldier and a responsible NCO till the time he served!

--*

I mentioned the psychological impact of a disciplinary march-up on a soldier in the previous story. Basically, even though the actual procedure of an individual getting marched-up, punished and marched out takes not more than five minutes, however, in the couple of days leading up to the march-up, it would be fair to assume that the individual would not be in a very happy state of mind.

In some cases, this loss of peace of mind is in itself adequate punishment commensurate to the act of indiscipline. This was one tool which I learnt to exploit fairly early during my command, especially in the case of young soldiers who were first time offenders and it would be far too early to have a permanent disciplinary entries on their records.

Hence, on quite a few occasions, such soldiers were made to go through the paces from being told that they would be marched up, getting requisite documents and charge-sheets, etc., prepared, to being actually formally marched up to the CO, only to be given a stern warning and being let off without any formal punishment.

The sense of relief on their faces was reward enough for me and the few days spent by them worrying about the march-up was punishment enough for them to learn from their mistakes!

As they say, the aim of the justice system is to reform, not punish. And these youngsters did get the message most of the time!

--*

Col Rakesh was the Tiger of one of the most decorated battalions of the Grenadiers Regiment. This happened about a week before he was to relinquish his command and hand over the reins of the Battalion to his successor.

One morning he got the message that the Military Police have caught one of his boys for some violation.

Upon hearing the name of the defaulter, Col Rakesh did a face-palm! The guy was a known problem child of the Battalion, and here he was, caught yet again.

But what annoyed Col Rakesh the most was that he was already in the midst of an emotional journey that the last few days of command are, and now he would have to deal with this latest misdemeanour of the guy as well.

Thankfully, the Military Police agreed not to file an official report and instead, let the Battalion take care of the matter.

However, time was short and this was something that Col Rakesh didn't want to leave for the next Tiger to deal with.

So he decided to try another approach.

He called the entire Battalion to assemble for a Special Sainik Sammelan by their outgoing Tiger.

Mind you, all this happened within an hour, right from getting the news of the guy getting caught, to passing orders for the Battalion to assemble.

It took about an hour for the Battalion to assemble.

Once they were all in, the Tiger took the stage and called the young defaulter to stand beside him.

The young lad, being a perpetual defaulter, seemed unconcerned, with even a hint of a smirk on his face.

Yet, his Tiger knew what he wanted of him.

The usual drill in the Battalion was that every address by the Tiger during a Sainik Sammelan would commence with a reading of the Grenadiers' Code by the Subedar Major. This time, however, Col Rakesh decided to change that drill a bit.

"Today, this soldier will read out the Grenadiers' Code", announced the Tiger.

(The Grenadiers' Code is a pledge of honour taken by all troops of the Grenadiers Regiment whereby they promise to do their best for the sake of the 'izzat' of their Regiment.)

The young defaulter thought he had gotten away lightly for what was a relatively major misdemeanour!

So he began reading out the Grenadiers' Code. Like all his fellow soldiers, he too knew it by heart and was just going through the motions of rattling it out, at least in the beginning.

But as he reached the middle part of the Code wherein the soldiers promise not to do any such act that will harm the 'izzat' of their Regiment, something clicked and he started crying uncontrollably in front of his Tiger.

Upon seeing the intended effect on the young lad, Col Rakesh concluded the Sainik Sammelan by saying a quick 'Thank You', followed by the Regimental War Cry as was the tradition and left the stage.

No other words were said.

No other words were necessary.

This simple, and different approach worked like no other punishment might have worked in this case. The defaulter realized his mistake and rendered a sincere apology, with a promise to try and become a better soldier of his Regiment.

Here was a Tiger who knew instinctively what needed to be done in that particular instance, given the circumstances. The young soldier, having learnt his lesson, was duly pardoned and life in the Battalion carried on without any further interruptions.

8

MIGHT AS WELL DO IT WITH A SMILE!

Discuss to the point of exhaustion.
But once a decision is given,
Put your shoulder to the wheel
And PUSH!

—**Source Unknown**

Many a time in life, you feel like tearing at your hair when faced with circumstances that are either plain ridiculous, or they need you to do something that goes way out of your comfort zone.

Like any other part of our society, the military too isn't immune to such things once in a while.

Herein comes the value of a good team for a *Tiger* who would essentially need to explain to them what needs to be done, and more importantly, WHY it needs to be done (in case someone asks!)

This happened with my battalion once in a small town in the foothills of the Himalayas where we were serving at that time.

To explain the context, the Battalion had already received orders to move to a high-altitude area under another formation and the *Advance Party* had already gone.

The *Main Body*, or the rest of the Battalion, was to move out on the first day of the following month which happened to be a Monday.

This incident that I narrate happened about two weeks before the day of the actual move. Suffice to say, the Battalion was in an insane *packing* mode and basically winding up our commitments all across.

With this as the background, I'll take you to the story.

One fine Monday morning, I got a call from one of the staff officers of my Brigade Headquarters that the responsibility for conduct of a *Diwali Mela* for the entire station is being given to my Battalion.

Best Part?

It was to be organized on the Saturday that fell two days before the final departure of the Battalion from the Station!

To be fair, the Brigade staff were quite apologetic since they too knew our situation. In fact, the Brigade Commander himself wasn't very happy about having to ask us to do this either. But then, such was the timing of the entire issue that a bulk of the local units were away from the station on various training commitments and we, having been excused due to our impending move, were the only ones available!

Needless to say, I wasn't in the best of moods when I broke this news to my core team of officers and JCOs.

As expected, there was a moment of silence as they all digested the magnitude of the task laid out in front of us.

And then my Subedar Major, Sunil *Saab,* spoke three words.

Hunchha Hajoor. Bhaiyalchha.

(Translation: *Roger Sir. Will be done*)

At this point in time, I cannot emphasize enough, the value of a good and mature Subedar Major, who is literally the Grand Old Man of the Battalion, being the senior most among all JCOs!

Sunil Saab had correctly deduced that the task could not be wished away. Instead, he took it as a way of bidding a Final Farewell to the Station by the Battalion. Of course, it was a given that the Battalion would put its best foot forward (as always!) instead of cribbing and doing a half-hearted job.

Suddenly, there was a discernible uplifting of mood in the Conference Hall. It took another hour or so of collective brainstorming before a broad plan was formulated. Since my 2iC had already moved ahead to the next place of deployment with the *Advance Party*, the Subedar Major was to be the main coordinator and accordingly carried on with the conference after I left to carry on with other engagements.

That evening, when I gave the daily report to my Brigade Commander, he once again enquired whether we would be able to manage the task. He even offered to speak with the Divisional Commander to get it re-assigned to someone else in case I felt we couldn't do it.

However, I was able to assure him that it would be done and offered a preliminary briefing at the site of the event after two days.

After initial representations to see if we could get out of having to do the task, there was to be no more arguing about the same. It was now not just a matter of principle, but of the Battalion's reputation. It was now time to put the shoulder to the wheel and PUSH!

Of course, the Brigade and Division Commanders had seen the battalion perform admirably over the past couple of years since they had been in the Station. The reputation that the Battalion had built up under my predecessor was quite solid indeed.

Such was the level of confidence instilled in me by my team that I could already commit to brief my own boss at such short notice without having to go back and ask those that were to actually execute the task at hand!

Anyhow, a core team was detached from the intricacies of the impending move of the Battalion and instead, dedicated towards the arrangements for the Station Diwali Mela that would see a footfall of close to 10,000 people.

Needless to say, the Brigade Commander was quite satisfied with the initial plans that were briefed to him by Sunil Saab himself. Of course the Brigade Commander did make it a point to express his regret at the circumstances that had forced him to give this responsibility to us. But the wise old man that Sunil Saab was, he just brushed it away gracefully by just pointing out the fact that orders were orders, and they would be executed to the best of our ability.

And then, as if to reiterate the Sunil Saab's point of doing it well, yet another JCO, Subedar Dhiren, suggested that we also organize a raffle, or a lucky draw!

And naturally, since it was a major, station-level event,

the first prize just *had* to be a bike, along with a couple dozen other prizes of varying value!

Yes, Subedar Dhiren had the entire thing planned out in his head and just needed a go-ahead to do it, in addition to all the other minor and major tasks for the event. And this, when he was also overseeing his own company's packing for the impending move!

As you might have guessed by now, Dear Reader, the Diwali Mela was a stunning success!

No excuses were offered by my men when it had come to organize the event when they would be moving out of the Station less than 36 hours later.

In my opinion, there were two reasons for this.

Firstly, they knew that in the larger scheme of things, they all (and indeed, I as well) were merely faceless masses of individuals that represented the much larger entity that our Battalion was, and continues to be. It was not the reputation of us as individuals that was at stake but instead, it was the reputation of the Battalion itself. Hence, there was just no way we wouldn't give it our best shot.

Secondly, (and I say it with full pride, humility and even *arrogance*, to some extent!) these troops from the Himalayan regions that comprised my Battalion, just didn't know how to underperform!

Now back to the Diwali Mela.

As I mentioned above, the event was a resounding success!

There were pats on the back for all the working hands by the Division Commander who made it a point to publically announce the efforts put in by my troops at a time when the Battalion was literally packed up for its permanent move.

Of course, there were congratulatory handshakes for me as well.

But looking back with the benefit of hindsight and a few more years added to my life, I can say confidently and more importantly, without any hesitation, that I received those pats and handshakes NOT because I had done a fantastic job, but because it was my Battalion that had done so.

I was merely the face of the Battalion for the world at large.

Yes, to some extent those congratulatory handshakes were justified because this also meant that in case of any failures or sub-par performance, it would be me as the *Tiger* who would be in the firing line and not my troops.

The buck always stops with the *Tiger*, whatever the outcome!

That said, I have no shame in acknowledging that on more than a few occasions, it was the Battalion that carried me rather than the other way round. In fact, dare I say, this was the case on most occasions.

The kind of goodwill that each and every single soldier earned for the entire Battalion was outstanding indeed, regardless of where they were employed/deployed.

And I was fortunate enough to have inherited such a wonderful body of men.

I'll end this story with a saying that I came across somewhere on the internet some years ago –*If the crowd starts walking in the right direction, 'leaders' will have no choice but to rush to the front!*

This, Dear Reader, is what a well-nurtured team can do for their leader. It can carry him far … much farther than he could ever reach alone.

Sunil Saab (left) in Good Cheer on the Day of the Diwali Mela.
The Hard Work was duly appreciated by all

The Lucky Draw Stash, Including the Motorcycle!

--*

Talking about not knowing how to underperform that I mentioned in the previous story, I'll just share an anecdote from my days as a young Lieutenant in the Battalion.

One fine day in the year 2003, we got orders that the Brigade was to field a handball team for the Divisional Championship and that the Brigade Commander would prefer to send a homogenous team from a single battalion.

With only two battalions available in the Brigade at that time, a friendly match was organized, with the winner expected to represent the Brigade. Of course, I was hastily appointed the Captain of my own Battalion Handball Team that too was equally hastily assembled!

But due to some other commitments, my CO wasn't too keen to detach 10 boys for a period of almost three weeks for the purpose.

Hence, before the match he quietly took me aside and told me as diplomatically as he could that we shouldn't win the match.

I too tried in all the bumbling diplomatic finesse that the 23-year-old me could muster and conveyed the same to my team.

I won't be wrong if I say that I could literally see the fuses in their heads get short-circuited!

They just couldn't fathom the concept of DELIBERATELY *losing!*

Yup, we went on to thrash the opposing team nice and proper. Perhaps even more than what we might have in case we hadn't been 'advised' to lose!

The CO too could only give an affectionate, all-knowing smile, since he too knew fully well as to why his orders weren't obeyed!

The Handball Team with the Brigade Commander after a Resounding Victory!

9

Empowered Subordinates Can and Will Surprise You!

The greatest leader is not necessarily the one who does the greatest things.
He is the one that gets the people to do the greatest things.

—Ronald Reagan

'The Buck Stops With Me', is the working principle of any half-decent *Tiger* because whether he likes it or not, it is a fact that ultimately it is he who is answerable for whatever happens within his Unit, or whatever is done by his Unit. And it applies both ways, for good deeds as well as for any slip-ups.

Now with nearly 800 free-thinking souls under your command, including quite a bunch that are physically quite far away from your direct influence, you really don't have a say in what will happen and when.

All you can do is to just hang on and ride whatever wave comes your way!

Almost everyone who has commanded a Battalion/ Regiment realizes this. Yet, in perfect sync with age-old wisdom that has been accumulated over millennia, here too we find different folks handling things differently, based entirely upon their personality and circumstances.

Some become micromanagers, while others assume more of a *Directive* style of command. Now I'm not being judgmental here and will just repeat that the way one chooses to command is not just a function of their personality, but of their circumstances as well.

When it came to circumstances, in my case particularly, I would say that I was dealt a rather kind and generous hand by the powers that be!

Not only did I get to command under excellent bosses (and excellent staff in their headquarters as well), but I also had a wonderful bunch of officers under me throughout my tenure, not just qualitatively but quantitatively as well!

I was blessed with a stream of excellent 2iCs as well as quite a bunch of youngsters and the relatively senior company commanders. Oh, and two doctors as well that were posted to me one after another by the virtue of the Battalion being in a challenging field area!

Each and every one of them brought something unique to the table and was worth his weight in gold.

They would happily fill in for each other whenever needed, and generally were a happy bunch, right from the senior most Lieutenant Colonel to the youngest Lieutenant. It is a testimony to this happy bunch that despite having a total of 18 officers under my command at one point in time, there was not even one single case of any inter-personnel issues or differences.

All that one needed to do as their *Tiger* was to just guide and channelize them in the correct direction.

Thankfully, this is all I did!

It was thanks to them and their hard work that I was able to have a relatively happy command and pursue other passions, such as writing.

What gave me this confidence in them was their abilities individually as well as collectively. Ironically, they themselves drew this confidence from my faith in them!

All in all, it was a self-fulfilling loop that we had created for ourselves; a loop which actually delivered whenever the going got tough.

I'll mention just one example when this team rose to the challenge as one and pulled off an incredible feat of skill and endurance, all in a day's work!

It so happened that one fine evening as I headed downhill towards the Station badminton court for my daily game, I got a call from my Adjutant, Tarun, that they had received reports that some vehicles were stuck at the SeLa Pass (which was about 8 km ahead of our Battalion location) and that he was moving out with a Quick Reaction Team for the rescue operation.

I gave him the go-ahead and also advised him ensure he remained in communication with the Unit doctor, just in case someone needed immediate medical care.

This happened at about 4 p.m.

This done, I merrily went about with my series of games for the evening, returning to the Battalion at about 7 p.m.

The rescue columns were still out, reported the Subedar Major, *including an additional one launched under Lieutenant Lavanya.*

Fine, I replied, *let me know when they return.*

Despite it being the month of March, the weather was still quite chilly. In fact the last few days had witnessed a renewed bout of pretty heavy snow which was also the reason why some vehicles were stuck at the SeLa Pass that was at an altitude of about 13,800 feet above sea level!

I wasn't quite worried about Tarun, Lavanya and the others that were up there. In fact, Tarun had actually requisitioned some more personnel to help cope with the situation in the vicinity of the Pass.

So I knew that they were on top of the situation and were just a bit delayed in sorting it out.

Periodic reports from the top via radio and by own vehicles bringing down rescued civilians for immediate medical assistance also indicated that things were under control.

I did think about going up and seeing for myself, but then decided against it because at this juncture, I suddenly showing up would divert the attention and efforts of the boys away from the immediate task at hand – that of rescuing the stuck persons.

Thus, it was an operation that was solely executed by Tarun and the bunch of youngsters, right down to the youngest rifleman who was part of the team.

That it was a major effort was becoming clearer by the minute as I kept on getting reports of evacuees reaching the ad hoc relief centre established by the Brigade Headquarters at a lower altitude, as well as a few critical cases that were coming to my own Battalion area for immediate medical care.

The rescue effort finally wound up at about 10 p.m. when the last of my boys were back in the Battalion location after physically ensuring that no other soul remained stuck in the snow.

Quite appropriately, a mug of hot soup and/or a couple of tots of rum had been made ready by the Subedar Major to help warm up the rescuers who themselves were freezing cold by now!

I too had delayed my own dinner and waited for Tarun and Lavanya to return so that they could eat with me in my room. I also decided to call the doctor to join us. This way I was also able to get a quick debrief of the efforts that had been put in over the past 6-8 hours as well as ensure that the boys were well fed when their dead tired bodies hit their beds!

A special situation report, or sitrep for short, was sent to the Brigade Headquarters by about midnight. The total tally we reported was 680 civilians rescued and about 300 vehicles recovered.

Thus ended a very long evening in the hills of Arunachal Pradesh! Sadly, two lives were lost – a seventy-year-old tourist from Gujarat and a woman cyclist from somewhere in Europe.

Next morning, when we took stock again, we realized that the effort had been even larger than what we had officially reported. The number of civilians rescued was close to 1,000, instead of the 680 that we had hurriedly calculated.

However, the actual figures were moot at this point of time because reports of a massive rescue operation at SeLa

Pass were already appearing on Social Media, thanks to some of those rescued who were posting about it.

This was eventually picked up by the National Media and by the evening, the Defence Minister's official handle too had tweeted about the same!

It was a well-deserved pat on the back for the youngsters who had just gone about their duty as part of 'All in a Day's Work'!

Once again, all the credit that I can take for this successful operation as the *Tiger* would be merely in letting my team test their own wings, with full confidence in their *Tiger's* own confidence in them.

Many Lives were Saved by the Boys

रक्षा मंत्री कार्यालय/ RMO India
@DefenceMinIndia

The Indian Army conducted rescue operation for 680 people stuck in the heavy snowfall at Sela Pass, Tawang, Arunachal Pradesh.
The operation was conducted in sub-zero temperatures at an altitude of 13,000 ft for more than seven hours without break.
@nsitharaman @PemaKhanduBJP

PIB India and 4 others

5:04 PM · Mar 13, 2018 · Twitter for Android

Tweet by Raksha Mantri

A Potential Disaster was Averted that Night

There was an interesting, serendipitous postscript to the epic rescue mission of that night, one that played out over the next few months and years. One of the vehicles whose occupants were rescued by Tarun included a young lady from Mumbai who took an instant liking to this dashing young lad who was risking his own health and life for them all!

Even as he concentrated on the rescue mission, she kept on beseeching him to share his phone number with her.

Our man Tarun was understandably a bit .. well .. let's say, shaken up at this sudden interest of hers, especially given the circumstances under which they had met. Very wisely, he managed to give her the slip by climbing further up to rescue those stuck at higher reaches.

Next, she tried to charm Lavanya into sharing Tarun's number with her. But Lavanya too was a smart cookie and chose not to, this time for the sake of his own health because he knew Tarun, who was not only senior but also outweighed him by more than just a fair margin, wouldn't be very happy if he did so!

She finally decided to make her way down to the Battalion location along with some folks in need of urgent medical attention and found herself in the Unit MI Room where the doctor, Capt Anjani, was doing his bit.

Of course, being the jolly prankster that he was, Anjani was quick to part with Tarun's number!

The story took a while to reach my ears via the 2iC during one of the evenings in the Officers' Mess. THIS was when I was finally able to put in context that unspoken communication that was happening between Tarun and Anjani on the night of the rescue when they had joined me for dinner!

Ultimately, less than two years after the rescue operation, Tarun got married to the younger sister of the lady who had so persistently sought his number that night!

Homeward Bound!

When the defining memory of home is immense physical separation from loved ones thanks to your profession, sometimes one needs a gentle reminder that home is not that far away. In the same spirit, one of my Battalion youngsters, Vineet, decided to design this distance marker and have it placed right outside the Gate Number 2 of the Battalion which was used by all the troops. Listed on the board are the locations from where most of our troops hail!

10

DISTRACTIONS ARE A MUST!

"All work and no play makes Jack a dull boy!"

Most professions in this world demand the utmost dedication from those who form part of them. However, once the day in the office is done, they go home to their own lives away from office and with their loved ones. This, in my opinion, is what helps folks retain a semblance of balance in life. Not only that, by taking the mind away from office for significant periods of time, it stays fresh for when you go back to work the next day or the next week.

It is more so in the profession of arms wherein, at least when deployed in field areas, there is no 'home' to go back to after work, so to say. In fact, the work-day itself is a daily, never-ending 24-hour cycle wherein your tasking rotates equally between daytime and night-time.

At times, especially during field tenures, monotony of routine sets in and instead of being ever vigilant, soldiers may end up going about the motions just like machines going about the same routine day and night.

Add to that the lure of the Smartphone and cheap data plans, and you have a real problem of 'dull boys' at hand, whether in the military or on the civvie street!

Hence, the need for distractions that not only give your active mind a rest, but also rejuvenate your spirits a bit!

Thus, it was a constant endeavour for me to get the boys out of the office and equally importantly, away from their Smartphones for at least a small part of the day. It was a challenge indeed due to circumstances that were quite ironical, if you can say that.

On one hand, we were billeted at a remote location at an altitude of 12,000 feet above sea level for most of the year, while on the other hand 4G mobile network coverage had recently become available there.

Then there were the few months every year wherein we would move for training in an even remoter location which was at an altitude of 14,000 feet, yet it too got some spill over of 3G coverage from a mobile tower some distance away!

All in all, despite the troops being naturally outgoing, it would at times still be an effort to keep them engaged in 'distractions', so to say. But an unanticipated bonus that accrued out of this unique challenge was the sheer number of different activities we were able to come up with because of it.

The activities included a cricket tournament at the large helipad near Brigade Headquarters, with practice sessions in the small flat area at the Unit location. There was a chess competition as well as an inter-company talent hunt. And then there was the one evening when I gathered all my officers in my hut for dinner and a session of playing video games over four different consoles!

However, the most intensely-fought competition amongst them all was also one that lasted nearly three months. It was the *Inter-Company Moustache Competition*!

You see, Gorkhas aren't exactly known for having facial hair, thanks to their genetics. But given the fact that their *Tiger* hailed from the lands of Punjab and despite a bald head, sported a thick moustache, it was only natural for me to institute this competition for an entire three-month duration that we were out for training.

The best part is that there was no structure to this 'competition'. All that I had passed by the way of my order was that there would be an Inter-Company Moustache Competition, and had just left it at that. This was partly to see how my flock responded and partly also because I myself hadn't given much thought as to how to orchestrate it!

But regardless, pretty soon, most of the boys in the Battalion had small tufts of hair underneath their noses!

It created quite a buzz, not merely in the Battalion, but in the entire Brigade, with my Gorkha lads bravely and as is their nature, cheerfully telling anyone who asked, that they were participating in a moustache competition. This also led to a lot of interesting conversations in the weeks and months that followed, even at the most unlikeliest of places.

In fact, I don't think we ever went about announcing any winner for that particular competition. But the three-odd months during which we all *competed,* were full of hearty laughter and other banter with respect to the progress of hair growth (or rather, lack of it) right under the noses of everyone!

So much so that even folks in the Division Headquarters, which was a two-day journey from the exercise area would often ask about the progress of the 'Moustache Competition' every once in a while whenever I or anyone else in the Battalion got a chance to speak with them.

That was fun!

By the way, an unexpected fallout of the 'Moustache Competition' was the discovery of Havaldar Khadka who was blessed with an excellent crop of facial hair! He soon became my Regimental Police Havaldar on the condition that he would keep a permanent 'Rajasthan Style' moustache to add to his persona as the guy responsible for keeping the discipline of the Battalion in check. Of course, whenever someone from a higher headquarters came visiting, Khadka was right there with me to welcome them. For someone who saw him for the first time, a diminutive Gorkha NCO with a huge moustache and an attitude to match was a novelty indeed!

Apart from the *Moustache* Competition mentioned above, another aspect of this personal endeavour of mine was the concept of self-development of my command.

Moving on, a popular saying in the military goes, *Busy Troops are Happy Troops.*

So, part of the efforts to keep them busy, especially in a field location without many avenues to channelize their energies, was to challenge them towards self-development.

The simplest way of doing so was to encourage everyone to read. Or, in my case, to *order* them all to read!

We had two different libraries within the battalion with close to five thousand books. While officers were given books hand-picked by me, all troops would pick up books of their own choice when proceeding on leave.

I am glad to report that in addition to those who already read books regularly, at least three more of my young officers made reading a habit thanks to me pushing them relentlessly. The rest read at least six books each during my command. On the other hand, my last Adjutant, Vineet, barely managed to read about a dozen pages of a single book despite all my encouragement and even threats! But then he was more interested in games and working out in the gym, so I guess that evened things out a bit!

Regular in-house talks and lectures too were a matter of routine. I myself was amazed at the kinds of experiences and pursuits that the troops had and were willing to share with the rest of us, which would otherwise have remained unknown to others.

Basically, it was all an effort to keep them gainfully engaged instead of spending more time than necessary with their mobile phones. Dare I say, I succeeded to some extent in quite a few cases.

This effort was born out of a desire to give back a bit to the organization in general and my troops in particular, thanks to whom I had been deemed worthy of being placed in command my Battalion when my time came.

This is true for practically anyone in any position of authority – a sacred responsibility to ensure the well-being and future growth of your subordinates upon whose hard work your own success depends.

Hav Raj Kumar Khadka with his Famous Moustache!

Some years after my command when I was a staff officer in a higher headquarters, my Corps Commander once remarked in an informal gathering that an order of the Commanding Officer of any Battalion is unquestionable.

I wanted to narrate the one instance when an order of my own was overruled and there was nothing I could do about it, but at that moment I chose not to narrate it. This pertained to our guy Havaldar Khadka who was my Regimental Police Havaldar that I talked about in the previous chapter.

He put in an excellent effort not only in maintaining the discipline of the troops but also the well-being of his moustache. Till the time he went on a month's leave after a duration of nearly six months in the Battalion, that is.

Upon his return, I found him standing in front of me in the Interview Parade with a sheepish grin on his face and NO MOUSTACHE!

I was aghast!

Even before I could ask, he blurted out – "Sir, my wife told me to shave it off and to never grow it again."

Well, that killed the matter then and there because here was an authority which even the Tiger of that NCO couldn't overrule!

11

SUNGLASSES!

"Discipline is the soul of an army. It makes small numbers formidable; procures success to the weak, and esteem to all."

—**George Washington**

Apart from 'having a large heart', another piece of advice that I got from my predecessor when I took over command of the Battalion from him was to be careful of what I said. He said that whatever I wanted *would* happen because for the troops any statement made by their *Tiger* would be as good as a command from him. It did take a while to register, but when it did, I must admit that I was humbled to the very core.

Come to think of it, this is the way any good army functions – unquestioning obedience is an absolute necessity when under fire because that is the only way to win a battle. When it is a question of life or death, an over-thinking mind can be an impediment as compared to a simple mind conditioned to instantaneously respond to an order by their superiors.

As a *Tiger,* this was indeed an onerous responsibility vested in oneself.

I will cite just one, light-hearted example of this from my own days in command. I do hope I am able make my point!

There was an instance wherein one of my boys came down with UV Ray poisoning in his eyes when he went up a hill feature at about 17,000 feet altitude during a patrol, without the protection of sunglasses. The unfiltered sunrays at that altitude reflecting from untouched snow did what they had to do and consequently, the guy was ordered confined to the dark innards of his tent for the next three days by the Battalion Doctor.

Thankfully, he made a full recovery.

However, in order to prevent any recurrence of this to anyone else, orders were passed that all troops would wear sunglasses at all times during the day while we were in the exercise.

But, over the next couple of weeks, a practical problem was encountered. Those joining in the exercise area from the main battalion location didn't always have sunglasses when they came over.

So the orders were modified and promulgated throughout the Battalion.

Each and every individual of the Battalion, regardless of his location, would henceforth be required to be wearing sunglasses from sunrise till sunset whenever outside his barracks!

And voila, pretty soon each and every soldier of the Battalion was wearing sunglasses throughout the daytime, right from the Tiger to the youngest rifleman!

Apart from ensuring that there were no more issues related to eyes at the higher altitudes, this also had two unanticipated consequences. Firstly, the boys managed to pick up some of the costliest and most fashionable sunglasses they could procure from anywhere and with the Gorkhas being gifted with a naturally smart physical disposition, they were pretty soon the smartest looking troops anywhere in the Corps Zone.

Secondly, well, the 'Sunglasses Wearing Battalion' pretty soon became the talk of the town everywhere right from the forward areas all the way up to the Corps Headquarters!

Then there was the matter of a further upsurge in the *josh* and morale of the boys at having a unique privilege that no other troops in the area had!

Yes, while the underlying reason for passing these orders remained, my troops took to it with the glee and energy that is so characteristic of a bunch of good soldiers anywhere in the world and made a virtue out of a necessity – that of being *different*!

After initial amusement, and in some cases, consternation at seeing troops wearing sunglasses while in uniform, people gradually started to accept this as a new normal, especially when realizing that the orders were passed due to a valid concern about the health of the men.

Of course, the boys played their role quite well too. I still remember the new Deputy Commander of the Brigade telling me one day that when he had newly joined in his appointment, he was taken aback at seeing my boys from a tactical guard at the Brigade Commander's residence wearing sunglasses while on duty.

He said that he couldn't help but ask the sentry right after he gave him a crisp salute, as to why he was wearing sunglasses while on duty.

The sentry simply replied, *"Sir, these are the orders of my Commanding Officer."*

The Deputy Commander recollected that he had no reply to this and he just said OK and continued on his way to his new office, duly chastened!

This, folks is the power of your word in any part of any organization that comes under you. This is not to say that you become a dictator to those under you. In fact, that would be the worst thing you could do with the trust reposed in you by the organization.

As the person at the helm of your unit, sub-unit or department, you wear two different hats – one that makes you the single point of contact with higher echelons for anything required of your unit, and the other that gives you an even onerous responsibility of ensuring that your unit/department is always geared to *happily* do whatever it is that they are mandated to do.

In fact the one definition of leadership that has stayed with me ever since I heard it first says that 'Leadership is the art of getting a body of people to happily do what you want them to do.'

The word *happily* in the above definition just about sums it all up. If one can ensure this, then there will be no looking back, come what may.

In a military, troops *will* follow your orders, come what may, with or without you actively looking after their wellness because that is how they are trained. But that doesn't take away the importance of empathy towards those below you, especially when they have taken a solemn oath to even put their very lives on the line at your command.

A happy team will apply themselves a lot better than one that just goes through the motions. And it will show in the overall output of your command, even to the higher ups.

So, my advice would be to always make an endeavour to strive towards a pursuit of happiness even as professional commitments remain paramount.

At the same time, use the *power* that comes with your chair/appointment wisely. As I said earlier in this chapter, your orders *will* fructify into action, whether good or bad. So be careful in what you say to your men. Deliberate with your staff or even your peers within the organisation before passing orders, in case you feel the need for external inputs.

As I close this chapter, I will try and underline the importance of understanding the impact of what you say in the short filler that follows next. With that, I shall rest my case at least in this particular aspect!

Once, when coming back to my Battalion after a particularly long conference at the Brigade Headquarters followed by a cup of tea with a fellow Commanding Officer in his Battalion, I saw the sentry at the gate still wearing sunglasses even though it was almost completely dark!

Naturally, I asked my driver to halt at the gate instead of merely driving through it as he would normally do.

The sentry was duly summoned and asked why was he was still wearing sunglasses when there was no need for it.

The young lad simply replied, "It is not yet 4:30 p.m."

It took me a moment before I realized that the orders for wearing sunglasses from dawn to dusk had been passed on further with a bit more specificity to mean from 4:30 a.m. to 4:30 p.m. With a change of season, sunset in our part of North-Eastern India was now at about 4 p.m.

Yet, here was this innocent young trooper who fully intended to keep his sunglasses on till 4:30 p.m. because those were the orders!

Needless to say, the order was suitable modified that very evening!

But on a more serious note, this is what makes them some of the best troops in battle – unquestioning loyalty and obedience. This is also what makes one strive really hard indeed in order to make oneself worthy of having such subordinates.

Sunglasses Galore!

12

INHERITED GLORY

Some goals are so worthy, it is glorious even to fail

**—Capt Manoj Kumar Pandey,
Param Vir Chakra (Posth)**

As I mentioned earlier in this book, I had the honour and the privilege of getting commissioned into, and later commanding, one of the most illustrious Battalions of the Indian Army – First Battalion The Eleventh Gorkha Rifles. This Battalion has earned the reputation of being a formidable fighting outfit through feats of bravery and sacrifice in the 1971, Sri Lanka and Kargil Wars, as well as during counter-insurgency operations in the North-East as well as in the Kashmir Valley.

This is not to say that other battalions of the Indian Army haven't been similarly valourous, but just to highlight that amongst the hundreds of battalions that make up this army of ours, mine has been one of the few that are immediately recognizable by some of the braves that have served as part of it.

The most well-known soldier amongst them is Captain Manoj Kumar Pandey, Param Vir Chakra (Posthumous), who laid down his life in the Kargil War. Another one, relatively lesser known is Lieutenant Puneet Nath Datt who earned a posthumous Ashok Chakra in July 1997, fighting terrorists in Kashmir.

Thanks to these two warriors, my Battalion is one of the barely handful that has been conferred the sobriquet 'Bravest of the Brave' to append to the name of the Battalion. This unique honour is awarded by the Indian Army to a battalion earning two of the highest gallantry awards that the Nation has to offer – the Param Vir Chakra and the Ashok Chakra. So exclusive is this club that the total number of battalions thus honoured is still in single digits.

Before I move on to what I mean when I call it 'Inherited Glory', let me tell you a story that helps underline what I have written above.

Sometime in the first week of January 2018 when I was commanding the Battalion somewhere in Arunachal Pradesh and located near the SeLa Pass, I got a call via my military exchange that an Air Force officer had called from Tawang, looking for me.

In the few moments that it took for my operator to patch through the call, my mind was in a spin as to what could be the reason for the call. Sadly, I couldn't fathom any probable reason, including why would an Air Force officer be in Tawang at this time of the year!

Shortly thereafter, the caller was on the line.

He introduced himself as the Defence PRO, Shillong.

Once again, I was confused! Why in the world would a Defence PRO be calling up, and that too when he is NOT in his given area of responsibility.

These doubts were, however, cleared pretty soon.

He told me that they were a group of three officers with their families who were on a road trip to Tawang. Enroute, they had crossed the Battalion location and seeing the name of Captain Manoj Kumar Pandey on the main gate of the Battalion (the gate was named after Captain Manoj Kumar Pandey), had decided to call me up on an army line once they reached their allotted army guest rooms in Tawang.

Apparently, two of the three officers in that group were coursemates of Captain Manoj Kumar Pandey.

Hearing this, I extended a quick lunch invite on their return journey. Two days later, the three officers along with their wives and kids arrived in the Battalion.

I kid you not when I say that neither they nor I felt it was a first meeting.

For them, it was nothing short of a pilgrimage to the 'Karmbhoomi' of one of their own; someone who had gone down in a blaze of glory nearly two decades earlier. For me, they were a medium to know more about someone who was my own inspiration, so much so that the story of his valour on the battlefield was the primary reason for me opting to put his Battalion as my first choice when I finished my military training.

At the cost of repetition, I will again say that the sheer number of young men opting to get commissioned into my Battalion right from my own time and even today, bears testimony to the kind of legend that Captain Manoj Kumar Pandey was, and continues to be.

It was a memorable afternoon, with they regaling us with the stories of their fallen coursemate. At the same time, they too got to rub shoulders with some of the war veterans who had fought shoulder to shoulder with Captain Manoj during the Kargil War.

Such impromptu visits happened on at least three occasions during my command, wherein such folks travelling towards Tawang saw the Battalion location enroute and decided to just walk in!

Such is the glorious name that the Battalion has earned for itself, thanks to valour on battlefield by our predecessors and the supreme sacrifices made by quite a few in the process. Most of those folks either fell in battle, or have long since retired.

This brings me back to the issue that I wanted to share in this particular chapter, that of *'Inherited Glory'*.

If you once again read what I wrote just before the last paragraph, you will notice that I used the word 'predecessors' when talking about the glorious name that my Battalion enjoys today. *This* is the key word on which this particular chain of thoughts is based.

I would always make it a point during my formal, monthly address to my troops during what we call in the Indian Army as *Sainik Sammelan,* that the glory and the wonderful name that the Battalion enjoys today has been earned by the sweat and blood of those who are no longer part of us, at least actively.

I would repeatedly emphasise this point each month that the glory in which we bask today ***was theirs to earn, but ours to lose*** if we don't put our best foot forward each and every time, whatever be the endeavour.

Yes, this is something that was always an underlying fear within me, and in fact, continues to this day as well. Those that earned this name for the Battalion have moved on and it is on the shoulders of the current generation that the onerous task of staying worthy of the laurels, rests.

You may want to re-read the last sentence in the paragraph above before moving ahead.

Each and every outsider that sees or visits the Battalion today, already has a basic understanding of our exploits in war. They come in, especially first-timers, including the ones I mentioned in the beginning of this chapter, not to see a Battalion being commanded by Colonel Harpreet Singh Kohli or those that have succeeded me subsequently. Instead, they come on a personal pilgrimage to visit the Battalion of their heroes such as Captain Manoj Kumar Pandey, Lieutenant Puneet Nath Datt or Colonel Lalit Rai.

For them, a person like me wasn't merely a Commanding Officer, but also a custodian of the indelible legacy of their heroes. And to be fair, I wouldn't blame them for looking at me this way either. Fact is that I too volunteered to get commissioned into the Battalion based on the same perception, without knowing much else about it.

Hence, my repeated exhortations to my troops to be extra cautious in their actions, because if they faltered, it wouldn't be 'Rifleman X' or 'Captain Y' that would be talked about, in case something went wrong. Instead it would be Rifleman X or Captain Y from Captain Manoj Pandey's Battalion.

Mind you, this is not to say that my troops were a bunch of indisciplined boys!

Nothing could be farther from the truth, in fact. They were, and continue to be, one of the finest bodies of fighting men that I have come across in my military career spanning a quarter of a century!

Our predecessors are the reason we earned this glorious name, and these current crop of men are the reason that we have been able to carry it forward without blemish.

It is always a good thing not to forget your past, but at the same time, to continue to march ahead into the future. Strong roots and a *will* to grow higher and higher are indeed a pre-requisite for any tree to thrive. The same is true for any organization as well. Devoid of even one of these two factors, an organization is likely to wither away sooner rather than later.

A good example of what I just wrote above would be the Kodak Corporation. They pioneered the development of digital photography and then, instead of adapting to the future, chose to hide it away so that their film business did not suffer! Resultantly, despite being the pioneers of the new technology, they went broke.

Here, I cap this particular chapter about what I realized as the *Tiger* when it came to matters of legacy and their impact on present as well as future endeavours. As the *Tiger* and consequently, a key custodian of our Inherited Glory, I look back with satisfaction that we were able to carry it on our shoulders with dignity, occasional mess-ups not withstanding!

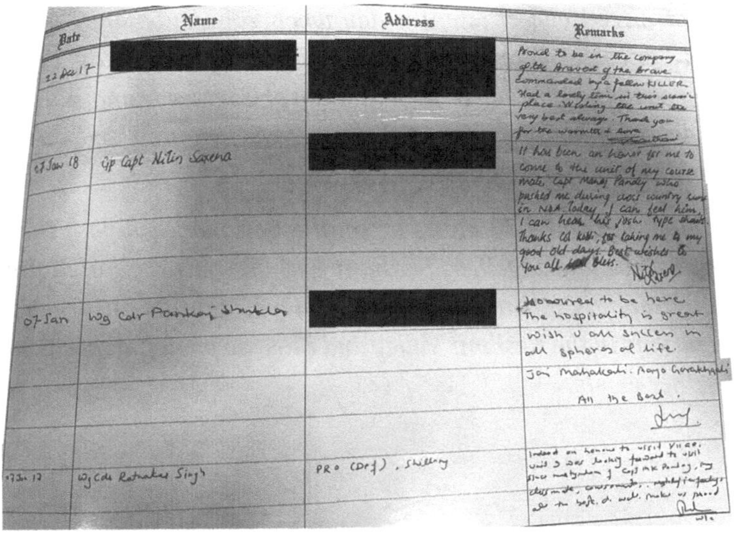

Date	Name	Address	Remarks
22 Dec 17	[redacted]	[redacted]	Proud to be in the company of the Bravest of the Brave commanded by a fellow KILLER. Had a lovely time in this scenic place. Wishing the unit the very best always. Thank you for the warmth & love. [illegible]
07 Jan 18	Gp Capt Nitin Saxena	[redacted]	It has been an honor for me to come to the unit of my course mate, Capt Manoj Pandey who pushed me during cross country runs in NDA. Today I can feel him, I can hear his josh type shouts. Thanks Col Kohli, for taking me to my good old days. Best wishes to you all. Bless. Nitin Saxena
07 Jan	Wg Cdr Pankaj Shukla	[redacted]	Honoured to be here. The hospitality is great. Wish u all success in all spheres of life. Jai Mahakali. Ayo Gorkhali. All the Best. [illegible]
07 Jan 17	Wg Cdr Ratnakar Singh	PRO (Def), Shillong	Indeed an honour to visit [illegible]. [illegible] looking forward to visit [illegible] Capt MK Pandey, [illegible] classmate, coursemate, [illegible] make us proud [illegible]

Remarks of the Coursemates of Capt Manoj Pandey in the Visitors' Book

In a strange twist of fate, the day when 2nd Lieutenant Puneet Nath Datt laid down his life in the line of duty (20 July 1997) was also the second day in the Battalion of Captain Manoj Kumar Pandey who had just reported after commissioning and initial orientation in the Regimental Centre.

Thus, for those 36 hours or so, the Battalion had both these heroes alive and together. Sadly, it was before the era of digital photography, and in the midst of intense counter-insurgency operations in the Kashmir Valley and thus, no photograph of them together exists.

When Another Decorated War Veteran of the Battalion Came Visiting: Major RV Ram, Sena Medal (Gallantry)

Little Samar Accompanied his War Veteran Grandfather to his Battalion

13

Bidding Farewell

The sweetest part of leaving home is knowing,
beyond the shadow of a doubt,
that you'll always carry it with you.

—(Unknown)

If I remember correctly, it was sometime in the end of 2018 when that year's Selection Board for the rank of Colonels took place. It was the Board that was to decide who in the Regiment would relieve me.

Consequently, as things shaped up, my earmarked reliever, Pankaj joined the Battalion in the last week of January 2019. Since he didn't originally belong to the Battalion, and was instead, from a sister battalion of the same Regiment, it was also for the reason of giving him time to settle down in the new Battalion and get to know the troops.

Being from the same Regiment, it was the same stock of troops as from his parent Battalion. Yet, each Battalion, even from within the same Regiment, is a unique entity, having its own *character*. This is why it was essential for Pankaj to get to know the pulse of the Battalion before he took over command from me.

Needless to say, it was my responsibility to groom my successor in order to ensure that he was able to deliver to the best of his abilities. Now, since almost everything about the Battalion was new for him, I did what I thought was the best thing to do – I proceeded on a couple of weeks' leave almost as soon as Pankaj reported to the Battalion and was declared medically fit to operate in the high-altitude location!

If you remember, my own predecessor, Col Chandran, too had done the same when I had returned to the Battalion after a long outing. I was merely carrying the tradition forward, so to say!

But jokes apart, this was a considered decision taken after due deliberation. My successor being in my shadow from the very first instance was something I wished to avoid, at least during the time he went about getting to know the Battalion and vice versa.

In fact, it would be better for the boys to look up to my successor as their next *Tiger,* rather than the current 2iC that he technically was. Hence, the decision to let him officiate in my absence from the very beginning.

Of course, a long-pending trip to Goa with the Better Half too was a factor in proceeding for a leave, conveniently coinciding with the marriage anniversary!

Anyhow, Pankaj soon settled in the Battalion. Meanwhile, I was in communication with the MS Branch at the Army Headquarters for my own posting. More than the place of next posting, I was interested in the timing of my moving out.

There was a reason for this. The Battalion had already received orders for moving to a peace station in Central India after having spent nearly two-and-a-half years in high altitude. The *Advance Party* was to move out in the last week of April, with the *Main Body* of the Battalion to follow a couple of months later.

In view of the above, my request to the MS Branch was to move me before the *Advance Party* left the Station. I wanted to bid farewell to the entire Battalion, including the personnel that were to form part of the *Advance Party.*

Consequently, sometime in the second half of February 2019, I received my Posting Order. As I had requested, the date given for relinquishment of Command was three weeks before the *Advance Party* would move. Hence, Pankaj too would have adequate time to prepare for the impending move after taking over.

I will take a moment here to talk about an aspect that might seem a bit ironical to some. However, those who have been *Tigers* in the Indian Army will definitely agree with me!

The thing is that psychologically, just as one is waiting in the beginning to assume command of their Battalion, similarly when one knows that the command tenure is coming to an end, there is a similar excitement while waiting for those orders!

To be fair, a tenure as a *Tiger,* though immensely satisfying in most cases, still entails shouldering a huge responsibility for a relatively long duration that would average about three years overall. At the end, one is actually looking to hand over the mantle to one's successor. In fact, the Battalion too requires an infusion of fresh blood to assume command, so that it continues to evolve!

Thus it was with me too when I received my orders.

And it didn't take long for everyone in the Battalion to find out either.

Needless to say, it created a buzz. This was because *Change of Command* is a major event for any Battalion anywhere in the Indian Army!

Pretty soon, Pankaj too got busy planning my farewell. But apart from that, life went on as usual since there was still work to be done and, of course, a Battalion to be commanded!

However, about 3-4 days later, it struck me.

'*This is it*', I realized. Not only would it be the end of the best phase of my military life thus far, but more than that, I wouldn't be coming back to serve in my Battalion with all these guys ever again. Henceforth, any visit would merely be as a *former* commanding officer.

It was sinking in rapidly.

Despite five-odd weeks still left for me as the *Tiger*, I was already nostalgic.

Nostalgic about leaving the Battalion.

Nostalgic about leaving home for good, in fact.

It was a mixed bag in those last few weeks. Routine training and administration activities carried on. What got added was a plethora of formal, semi-formal as also informal *farewell* parties and functions. To be fair, I too had hosted all outgoing *Tigers* in my vicinity, when it was their time to move on. You see, being a *Tiger*, with all the associated glamour and responsibility, is still a very lonely job.

It is not without reason that they say 'It is lonely at the top'!

Hence, over time, fellow *Tigers* become a fairly tight-knit group of peer confidants who are relied upon for professional advice, some socializing without any protocol issues, as well as sounding boards for ideas and of course, letting off steam whenever things overwhelm you!

So on and on I went, from one invite to another!

Yet, in the midst of it all there continued to be that nostalgia which I talked about earlier. I still can't quite define that feeling, even four years down the line as I type out this part of the book. What I remember is a sense of a looming emptiness slowly creeping in. Mind you, it was a sense of *impending* emptiness since I still had a few weeks to go.

Don't get me wrong, though. I still wanted to move on because that's the way military life is. Yet, this move would actually define the end of something that had always been a fact of life for me – of knowing that the Battalion was always there for me to return to, no matter how hard or difficult a particular posting might be.

It would no longer be the case now.

Okay, I think I have made my point by way of the longish rambling above! But then, my excuse is that I still am unable to find words to describe that feeling of the last few days and weeks as the *Tiger!*

But moving on, I decided to actually *plan* my own farewell.

I understand that the above statement sounds a bit ironic, so I will try and explain it a bit. As I think I have already brought out earlier in the chapter, leaving command of a battalion is an emotional roller-coaster ride. Somewhere along this ride, it dawned on me that there were some things that I wanted to do on my way out, including a specific type of memento that I wanted, in addition to the one traditionally given by the Battalion to outgoing *Tigers.*

It might sound a bit selfish to some, but then I can live with it!

That said, I will still offer an explanation. Firstly, I had absolutely no doubts that my flock would be doing their best to organize a befitting farewell for me. But then, I also knew that they aren't *mind-readers*! Hence, my decision to request Pankaj to discuss the farewell plan with me about a week before I was to leave.

This helped me suggest one or two things that I wanted incorporated as part of the farewell within the broad programme that he had prepared.

Why I did this was so that when leaving, I didn't go with a feeling of something being amiss in the final days. It wouldn't be the fault of my successor had that happened, mind you. He would still do his best but, like I said, he still wasn't a mind-reader! So it would just be me that would be to blame if I didn't find the farewell to be the way I had *imagined* it to be!

In any case, my suggestions just boiled down to a minor change in the drill in one of the formal functions and, of course, the specific memento that I wanted!

Time flew by, as usual, and the last week with me as the *Tiger* dawned soon enough. Thankfully, it was an affair that keeps you mighty busy, with a lot of social as well as professional requirements that need to be sorted out before leaving.

And then the inevitable happened!

About three days before handing over command to Pankaj, I was going down to the Brigade Headquarters for some work. It was hardly a five-minute drive. But almost as soon as my vehicle left the Battalion's main gate, I had a lump in my throat.

With the few minutes of peace that my active mind found during the short drive, all pent-up emotions came running to the surface.

Thank God I was wearing my sunglasses at that time!

In a way, that sudden and unexpected surge of emotions ended up being quite therapeutic. I could finally bring my focus back on the actual event instead of the daily grind of all the minor (and major!) activities that were leading up to it.

Strangely, I found myself quite at peace after that moment, and actually prepared for my departure. When the ultimate moment to finally leave the Battalion that I had called home for nearly two decades (and still call it thus!) came, I was prepared and in good spirits.

Pankaj was the one who drove the vehicle that was decorated by the troops for my farewell, just as I had done for Col Chandran about 34 months ago.

A tonne of photographs were taken before I finally was on my way, leaving *home* behind, smiling, because tears had already been shed a couple of days earlier.

Thus ended my journey as the 24th *Tiger* of a Battalion that has earned the highest glories in war as well as in peace. Whatever has come my way since, and will come my way ahead is all a bonus because having commanded my men, the work of my life was well and truly done.

I will end this chapter with some advice that I offered Pankaj. First and foremost was the advice given to me by Col Chandran that I found to be extremely useful and thus, I dutifully passed on to my successor as well – *Have a Large Heart*. That done, I added a few of my own, thanks to my experiences. These were:

> *Enjoy your time as a Tiger. This time will never come back!*
>
> *For the next six months or even beyond, if you find someone questioning you about anything that might have gone wrong, feel free to blame it on your predecessor, i.e., Me!*
>
> *And, of course, when your time is up, don't forget to plan your own farewell!*

BIDDING FAREWELL TO HOME

A Happy Family!

14

PARTING NOTES

As I come to the end of this book, the first thing I deem necessary to say is that this is not a *self-congratulatory* book, just in case it appears to be so to anyone. This is, instead, an attempt to chronicle what have been the best days of my military life thus far and the lessons I learnt from the most unlikeliest of the people under most unlikeliest of circumstances in many instances.

I made mistakes too, along the way. I did things that cannot be undone and I said words that cannot be taken back now. But looking back, I prefer to think of them as mistakes which taught me valuable lessons which I otherwise might not have learnt. Yet the guilt of having hurt someone in the process will stay with me till the very end. With this book, I hope that at least a few folks might learn from my mistakes and avoid making them all over again.

All said and done, *Being A Tiger* was a nearly three-year-long *high* that I was fortunate to be blessed with. It was a totally new and uncharted journey along the path of self-discovery and personal growth.

All of us who have been lucky enough to command battalions and regiments will agree that each *Tiger* has a unique journey, mostly based on their own experiences and circumstances. However, one common thread that still binds all these journeys together is the acknowledgement that it is indeed a privilege to be granted command of a body of men who are willing to put themselves in the path of mortal danger at your command.

I realise that I have mentioned this aspect of your men putting their lives on the line for you on more than a few occasions in this book. I think it is appropriate that I delve upon this for a moment before moving ahead to close this chain of thoughts.

Going by what you might have read thus far in this book, I am sure you realise that such *'life or death'* situations aren't a daily occurrence in military life. Heck, I would go on to say that some folks might actually complete their terms of service and even retire without finding themselves in such circumstances because wars don't happen as often and even the internal challenges facing the Nation are on the wane.

However, should the moment come, it is expected of the military man to unquestioningly follow his leader into the face of danger. *Follow Me* is the ultimate command that tests the very mettle of this relationship between the leader and the led.

For the leader, it is the sacred duty to ensure that when the time comes, he is right there with his boys, facing the same dangers and hardships as them, while for the led, it is the implicit trust that not only will their leader be there with them till the very end, but he will actually *lead* them to victory.

Examples of such leaders abound in the rich military history that the Indian Armed Forces have accumulated. The men of 3 JAT had clear-cut orders from their Tiger, Lt Col Desmond Hayde during the 1965 War as they went into the Pakistani town of

Dograi. They knew that they simply <u>had</u> to be at Dograi the next morning, dead or alive. Why? Because this was the simple order given to them by their Tiger. Also told to them was that in case the Tiger himself was wounded or killed in action, they were to physically lift his body and plant him at Dograi with them.

Needless to say, the Jats fought an epic battle that night and ensured that the Tricolour was flying in Dograi the next morning. Eighty of them gave up their lives in the process. All because they <u>had</u> to be in Dograi that morning because their Tiger had ordered them to.

Similar was the case with Lt Col Tarapore of 17 HORSE who went into battle with his men in the same war and spearheaded a deep thrust into Pakistan. He was right there with his boys, fighting, and gave up his own life in the war, leading from the front.

Then there is the story of Capt MN Mulla of INS Khukri who chose to go down with his ship instead of abandoning it, because he knew some of his crew would not be able to make it out alive. So much so, that he even gave his own life jacket to one of his boys after giving the command to abandon ship. He made the conscious decision of going down with those of his crew that weren't able to save themselves.

In fact, writing about her father nearly four decades after he went down with his ship, Mrs. Ameeta Mulla Wattal wrote that when she first heard of the sinking of INS Khukri, "I recall that my mother felt a hopeless despair because she knew that her husband would not put his own safety before the safety of his men."[4]

---

4. *Why They Chose to go Down with the Ship,* Ameeta Wattal Mulla. *The Indian Express,* 9 December 2010, http://archive.indianexpress.com/news/why-they-chose-to-go-down-with-the-ship/722341/

Of course, the story of Lt Col Brahmanand Awasthy, to whom this book is dedicated, is no different either.

Now these men didn't just get out of their offices one fine day and asked their boys to follow them. On the contrary, they had expended time and energy in *earning* this dedication and unquestioning loyalty from their troops in the many years leading up to the ultimate moment of glory and sacrifice. And when the time came, they unhesitatingly took the first step ahead, with full confidence that they wouldn't have to look behind to check if their men were following them.

The sign of a good leader is visible in every aspect of his Battalion/Regiment's functioning. A *Tiger's* personality invariably reflects in his command, be it during peace or war. No better example of this exists than in the 1971 War wherein we had General Sam 'Bahadur' Manekshaw on one hand and the self-appointed Field Marshal Yahya Khan on the other. No wonder that the Indian Army was able to decimate their Pakistani counterparts in an epic campaign that can only be described as a *Blitzkrieg without Tanks*!

The same is also true for other organisations as well.

So, as a *Tiger,* in case you find your own Unit lacking in some respect, just remember two things – firstly, look within yourself, and see what *You* can do to ameliorate the situation; and secondly, *do* what needs to be done!

You are in a unique position to effect the changes you want, at least in your own sphere of influence that is your Unit, even if circumstances outside are beyond your control.

As I conclude this book, I am reminded of one final

instance, befittingly at the very end of my days in command of my Battalion. During my *Dining Out* in the Brigade Officers' Mess, my Brigade Commander remarked (in some context that I am unable to recollect now) that a command tenure need not be happy, so long as it is a successful one. When the time came for my own farewell speech, I started by saying that I wasn't quite sure whether my command would count as a successful one or not (since that is mostly a function of hindsight), but I knew for sure that I thoroughly enjoyed each and every moment that I was in command of my Battalion!

In the end, all I will write is a quote that I read somewhere. Even though not applicable specifically to the military, I have found it to be a good guiding *mantra*. Here it is:

People don't quit bad jobs. They quit bad bosses.

My Flock. Forever Indebted to Them All

A Tribute to a Mentor

Subedar Major (Honorary Captain) Sunil Kumar Limbu was the Battalion Subedar Major when I assumed command. Quite literally the 'Grand Old Man' of the Battalion, he had more or less seen all that there had to be seen.

Consequently, his gentle but firm advice, whenever needed, was something that was worth its weight in gold and couldn't be ignored. A mature and professional soldier, he had a firm grip on all affairs of the Battalion.

In his own way, he too played a key role in moulding me as a *Tiger* in my initial days of command.

Behind his ever-smiling and jolly persona was a soldier who had seen war in all its brutal glory. He had joined the

Battalion during operations in Sri Lanka as part of Operation Pawan. Taking part in all subsequent operations as well, he had taken three bullets in his body during one of the bloodiest assaults mounted by the Battalion in the highly critical days of the 1999 Kargil War. As a result, he was practically bedridden for almost two years.

Even though the doctors had written him off as disabled, he refused to give up and through sheer willpower, got walking and functioning reasonably 'normally' again. It was a long struggle that lasted nearly a decade. He ultimately rose to the very zenith of his profession before retiring.

Despite having hung up his boots in March 2017, in retirement too, he took it upon himself to be at the forefront of veteran affairs in his local community. In addition, he made it a point to stay in touch with whatever the Battalion was up to, and was also occasionally sought out by me for advice as and when needed.

In May 2021, this grand old soldier finally lost the battle to a virus that had plagued the entire world.

He is still missed.

About the Author

Col Harpreet Singh Kohli is a serving officer of the Indian Army. An avid writer, he has authored four books – *'The Autobiography of a Killer, 'The India-Pakistan Tango', 'The Other Side of a Soldier'* and *'Being a Tiger'*.

When the Tiger Himself is Bald, he can Insist on a Photograph
with all Bald Men of his Battalion!